TIME MANAGEMENT

Second Edition

Proven Techniques for Making Every Minute Count

Identify Strengths • Prioritize Objectives • Train Effectively • Control Finances • Resolve Differences

Richard Walsh

Adams Small Business Series
Buying Your Own Business, Second Edition, by Russell Robb
Management Basics, Second Edition, by John and Shirley Payne
Presentations, Second Edition, by Gary McLain
The Small Business Valuation Book, by Lawrence W. Tuller

Available through your favorite bookseller.

BUSINESS
Avon, Massachusetts

Published by Adams Business, an imprint of
Adams Media, an F+W Publications Company
57 Littlefield Street, Avon, MA 02322. U.S.A.
www.adamsmedia.com

ISBN 10: 1-59869-765-X
ISBN 13: 978-1-59869-765-0
Printed in the United States of America.

J I H G F E D C B A

Library of Congress Cataloging-in-Publication Data
is available from the publisher.

This publication is designed to provide accurate and authoritative
information with regard to the subject matter covered. It is sold with
the understanding that the publisher is not engaged in rendering legal,
accounting, or other professional advice. If legal advice or other expert
assistance is required, the services of a competent professional person
should be sought.
—From a *Declaration of Principles* jointly adopted
by a Committee of the American Bar Association
and a Committee of Publishers and Associations

Many of the designations used by manufacturers and sellers to distinguish their product are claimed as trademarks. Where those designations
appear in this book and Adams Media was aware of a trademark claim,
the designations have been printed with initial capital letters.

This book is available at quantity discounts for bulk purchases.
For information, please call 1-800-289-0963.

Contents

Introduction

An exact-phrase search for "time management" yields nearly 7 million results on Google and more than 9 million hits on Alta-Vista search engines. A search for "time management" in Amazon books returns more than 65,000 results. There are thousands of time management workshops and seminars.

Clearly, time and the management of time is an important issue, and the supply of time management products—books, articles, CDs, workshops, etc.—reflects the huge demand for these products. The proliferation of time management aids points out how commonplace time pressures have become, and how people are struggling desperately to cope with and find time for the demands placed on them.

Why do so many people have so much trouble managing their time? We are to blame, in part, for creating our modern lifestyle. We believe that a full life is a busy life, with work, family, hobbies, civic duties—all of which place real and conflicting demands on our time.

Many of us believe that the answer to this problem lies in compressing more activities into each day—having more things to do than there is time in which to do them is a problem that can be solved by becoming more efficient. If you have ten things on a typical day's to-do list and normally finish only five of them, then figuring out how to do six is a productivity increase of 20 percent. That's great if you're comfortable not doing four things. But that's not time management.

Some people believe that the answer is to apply more time doing those ten things. If they're work-related tasks, then, obviously, it's necessary to spend more time at work. Because time cannot be created, however, and only reallocated, spending more time on one activity means spending less on another. So, spending more time at work is great if you don't have a family, any relationships, hobbies, personal interests, or need sleep. But that's not time management either. At least it's not healthy time management.

Time management is activity management and involves defining what tasks need to be done and finding a realistic way in which to do them. Having more tasks to do than time in which to do them ensures failure. And having so much to do that you spend your entire waking life ticking off items from your to-do list will lead to frustration and burnout.

> *No man ever said on his deathbed, "I wish I had spent more time at the office."*
>
> —Senator Paul Tsongas

Within this book I'll discuss how to approach and complete tasks—those that are work-related, and those that involve family, friends, and community. These two worlds, if it needs to be said, are in different universes. The goal of the book is to help you deal with continuing time demands with common sense and efficiency so that what is most important receives its due.

Finally, you can read this book from start to finish, but that's not essential to understand its concepts. Instead, use the Contents to find a chapter about a topic of concern. Choose the subjects that are appropriate to your situation and help you the most. Good luck.

CHAPTER 1

Is Time Out of Control?

We listen in astonishment to the most severe examples on news broadcasts: stories involving someone who becomes so outraged over a seemingly trivial event that he assaults and injures or even kills another person. Road rage is one of the most common manifestations of this disorder, but there are many others and can involve almost any human activity. All that's required are two or more people, a spark, and a participant who takes the whole thing way too seriously. And it appears that these ingredients are available and come into contact with each other with surprising frequency.

These are extreme manifestations of what is typically referred to as "hurry sickness," a state of anxiety caused by the feeling of not having enough time in the day to accomplish everything that is required. Some people are so intent upon achieving their goals, that any disruption, even the ordinary, everyday kind, can send them into a homicidal, unthinking rage. We wonder how these people can lose control so quickly and completely, and are comforted knowing that we are more rational, more balanced, and better adjusted. We are unaffected by minor interruptions, and are in complete control of our emotions and actions.

Are we, really? While most of us, thankfully, are not prepared to commit mayhem when things don't go our way, many of us have a serious problem dealing with events that knock us off course, interfering with our goals. We are a nation of overachievers, with lives stuck on fast forward. With little time to plan, many of us have become adept at crisis management, rushing to put out one fire after another. We're all dependent on overnight delivery and communicating via e-mail, fax, and telephone. We're constantly connected by personal digital assistants and BlackBerries, and we time our commitments to the minute so that we can fit them into our crowded schedules.

> *Now, here, you see, it takes all the running you can do, to keep in the same place. If you want to get somewhere else, you must run at least twice as fast as that!*
> —Lewis Carroll (1832–1898) English author,
> *Through the Looking Glass*

Here's a simple test to see if you're suffering from hurry sickness. All you need is a partner to keep track of time while you estimate how long it takes for one minute to elapse. Sit down and get comfortable. No fair peeking at a watch, or counting off "One Mississippi, two Mississippi. . . ." To start the test, your partner says, "Go." When you think a minute has passed, you say "time's up!"

Go ahead and try it.

How far did you get? Did you underestimate the amount of time you had waited? If so, you're in the majority. In monitored tests, most folks called out "time's up!" after only about fifteen seconds. At least one subject thought the minute was up after just seven seconds. Very few made it a whole minute.

If we were as bad at estimating space as we seem to be at estimating time, we'd be crashing into each other all the time.

Here's another test. Just sit still and do nothing for one minute, sixty seconds, while your partner times you. How long does that minute of enforced inactivity seem to you? Are you uncomfortable with just one minute of stillness?

A minute has become an eternity. Now we measure time in nanoseconds, one billionth of a second. Super computers perform operations measured in "teraflops" or trillions of calculations per second.

One more test. It takes a little longer than the one-minute drill, but it isn't difficult, and it doesn't require a partner. Simply leave your watch at home when you go about your business tomorrow. At the end of the day, reflect on these two questions.

1. Did you find yourself checking your wrist even when you didn't want or need to know what time it was?
2. Even without your watch, did you have any trouble keeping track of time?

If you answered "yes" to the first question and "no" to the second, you're again in the majority. Most of us have become accustomed to tracking time in ever smaller increments as we drive ourselves from task to task, deadline to deadline, appointment to appointment. We even schedule the fun stuff. This constant checking has become habitual, so we don't even realize how time-driven we've become.

In our culture the trick is to *avoid* knowing what time it is. Reminders are everywhere. Clocks leer down at us from office walls, and watches bob on the wrists of almost everyone we meet. The fellow on the radio chirps out the time constantly, in artless variations. ("It's seven sixteen, sixteen minutes after the hour of seven o'clock, forty-four minutes before eight. . . .") Our computers flash the time at us when we log in and keep track of every passing minute while we work. Neon signs blink the time and temperature at us as we drive to our next appointment.

Pause for just a moment to consider this: at one time there were no clocks and no watches. When the first public clock was erected in a village in England, folks flocked to the town square to view the wonder. And it only had one hand! You could tell time only to the nearest hour.

Can we even imagine life without the timekeepers? Probably not. We're not just aware of time, we're driven by time, besotted with time, engulfed in time.

RIDING THE ADRENALINE HIGH

Here's another simple test to diagnose a possible case of hurry sickness. Just respond "yes" or "no" to the following statement: "I work better under pressure."

A lot of us seem to think so. We claim the trait on our resumes (along with "highly motivated self-starter"), and we brag about our ability to perform under the tightest of deadlines.

Some of us pick up this habit in college, waiting to write that term paper until the day before it's due, pulling an all-nighter, and going to class bleary eyed, bedraggled, but smugly self-satisfied that another challenge has been successfully met. Knowing how clever we are, we carry over the habit to other areas of our lives and press forward confident and hopeful that others will recognize our talents as well.

You, too? Go back and look at that work after you've calmed down. Your best? If you're honest with yourself, you'll admit that the quality of the work suffers when you race through it.

And *you* suffer, too. You've got motion sickness—not the kind that causes queasiness when you react to the rolling of a ship, but rather a physical and psychological dependence on motion and speed that can become almost as powerful as a true addiction.

"Leisure time" has become an oxymoron. We experience one long workday, broken but not relieved by gulped meals and troubled sleep. Only the models in the clothing catalogs seem to have time to lounge.

We Americans take shorter and fewer vacations, and we take our work with us, with our beepers and cell phones, faxes and e-mail. Our home computers are extensions of the office, but being able to work at home means that we're always at work.

Leisure is not as leisurely as it once was, and we race through life checking the "fun" items off the to-do list. Even our play has become purposeful with physical conditioning or enforced "relaxation," and competitive pastimes (who plays golf without keeping score?). Even birdwatching has become a competitive sport.

SIMPLE SYMPTOMS AND SCARY CONSEQUENCES OF HURRY SICKNESS

How about you? Have you got a case of hurry sickness? Symptoms include:

- nervousness
- depression
- fatigue
- appetite swings
- compulsive behavior (repetitive actions that are difficult or even impossible to stop)
- unwillingness and even inability to stop working
- inability to relax even when you do stop working

That's not good, but it's not lethal. Hold on. It gets worse. We all have to run the occasional sprint, meet the unyielding deadline, cope with the unforeseen emergency. And we can do so effectively and without long-term damage. It can even be exhilarating.

But keep driving in that fast lane until it becomes a way of life and you run the risk of:

- hypertension
- heart disease
- migraines
- insomnia
- digestive problems
- stroke

The stress of rushing through life suppresses the immune system, hampering the natural formation of T-lymphocytes (white blood cells) and leading to increased susceptibility to infection and cancer.

Life in the fast lane can make you sick. It can even kill you.

REPORTS OF THE "DEATH OF WORK" PREMATURE

In an article in a 1959 issue of *The Saturday Evening Post*, highly regarded historian and social commentator Arthur Schlesinger, Jr., warned Americans of "the onrush of a new age of leisure." Warned? In 1967 noted sociologists came before a U.S. Senate subcommittee on labor to predict with great confidence that Americans would soon be enjoying a twenty-two-hour work week or a twenty-two-week work year. Many of us would be retiring at thirty-eight, these experts said, and the big challenge, as Schlesinger indicated eight years earlier, would be in handling all that free time.

These prognostications remind me of the executive at Decca Records who turned down the chance to sign a garage rock band from England because "guitar music is on the way out."

The band was The Beatles, and they did *okay* with three guitars and a set of drums. The only one on the way out was the Decca exec.

How could the "experts" have been so wrong? What happened? Why didn't our marvelous technology usher in the Age of Leisure?

We took the money. We opted for a higher material standard of living instead of time off.

You don't remember making that choice? Perhaps it was never offered to you, at least not in those terms. But by and large most of us decided to work more rather than less, and more of us went to work, so that instead of the Age of Leisure we created the Age of Anxiety and the norm of the two-income household.

Women, in particular, got caught in the time crunch. You were supposed to be able to have it all, a thriving family and a successful career. But too many superwomen came home from a hard day at the office only to find all the housework waiting for them. They wound up working, in essence, a double shift, all day, every day. And single mothers never had a choice. If they didn't do it, it didn't get done.

Whether or not we made the choice consciously, there was plenty of pressure on us to choose the money. And it paid off; our standard of living rose as our incomes increased, and now every household is jammed with appliances, electronics, and . . . stuff. We want just about everything that's new and discard whatever's broken, worn, or just out of style with such frequency that our landfills are overflowing.

Hard workers get and keep jobs as well as social approval and disposable income. When the boss advises us to "work smarter, not harder," she really means "get more done," and that means working harder as well as smarter. "You can do more with less," we're told when asked to take over the workload for a departed colleague (no doubt a victim of "downsizing," or even "rightsizing"). But it's a lie. You can't do more with less. You can only do more work with more time, effort, and energy, and that time, effort, and energy have to come from other parts of your life—like conversation, sleep, and play.

WE HAVE SEEN THE ENEMY, AND IT IS US

Is it all the bosses' fault? Not really. In many ways we've inflicted hurry sickness on ourselves.

We use our busy-ness as a measure of our self-worth and importance. We define our sense of purpose and our meaning in terms of our to-do list. We've internalized the clear social message that busy people are worthy people, even morally superior people. ("Idle hands are the devil's workshop.")

It isn't just peer pressure. Deep down inside us, stillness makes us nervous. Many of us actually dread free time and secretly look forward to Monday morning (although we'd never admit it). Unstructured time is threatening, and so we fill up the hours—all of them.

We abhor the notion of "wasting" time and speak of "saving" time, and "spending quality time," as if, as the adage has it, time were money, or at least a commodity like money, capable of being either stashed or squandered.

"Half our life is spent trying to find something to do with the time we have rushed through life trying to save."

—Will Rogers (1879–1935),
American humorist and philosopher

So where is that "time" you've "saved"? You can't see it. You can't hold it in your hands. You can't put it in a box and hide it for safekeeping.

JUST WHAT IS TIME, ANYWAY?

"If no one asks me, I know," St. Augustine once replied to this question. "If they ask and I try to explain, I do not know."

Here's a simple way to find out what time is to you. Jot down several phrases that use the word "time" in them. Make them descriptive of the way you relate to time. For example, you might write:

"I'm trying to learn to spend my time wisely," or
"I've found that I can save time by making a to-do list every
   morning before work," or
"I tend to waste time after dinner."

Go ahead and take a moment to write a few. (This book is all about you working out *your* relationship with time. I promise the exercise has a point.)

Now rewrite each statement, but substitute the word "life" for the word "time" and see what you come up with.

In our examples above, we'd get:

"I'm trying to learn to spend my life wisely."
"I've found that I can save life by making a to-do list."
"I tend to waste life after dinner."

The point to this little parlor trick? (Did you think of it as a "waste of time"?) If even one of your revised statements startled you, even a little bit, you got the point. We aren't talking about some tangible commodity when we discuss the time of our lives. We're talking about our very lives. We no more "have" time than we "have" inches of height.

Time is nothing more (or less) than a way of measuring out our lives. Other cultures measure time other ways, and some cultures don't measure it at all.

Here are how some other cultures speak of time:

"Think of many things. Do one." —Portuguese saying
"Sleep faster. We need the pillows." —Yiddish saying
"Haste has no blessing." —Swahili saying
"There is no hand to catch time." —Bengali saying
"Today can't catch tomorrow." —Jamaican saying

And here's our own beloved bard, William Shakespeare, advising us from a long-gone time: "O, call back yesterday, bid time return!"

Can't be done. So, how "much" time do you really "have"? In one sense, we each have exactly the same "amount." We have the moment we're living right now. That's all. And it's everything.

That's not to say we shouldn't learn from the past and plan for the future, even if we can't store it or hold it. We're going to do a great deal of learning and planning as we explore time together. However, although we remember the past and envision the future (both highly creative acts), we can't live in either one of them.

You can only live as well as you can in the *now*. This book is designed to help you do that, and you have more choice in the matter than you think. To a great extent, you get to decide how you live right now.

You can use this basic checklist, four questions to help you make those decisions:

1. What has to be done?
2. What has to be done first (what's most important)?
3. How much of it has to be done?
4. How fast does it have to be done (what's the deadline)?

The answers to these questions will enable you to decide what to do now. These decisions will add up to your whole life, well lived.

CHAPTER 2

Are You Really as Busy as You Think?

Are you working longer and harder now than you used to? You said "yes," right? Most people do—especially those who buy books on time management.

Juliet Schor agrees with you.

In her 1991 bestseller *The Overworked American,* Schor notes that the shrinking American work week bottomed out at 39 hours in 1970 before it started to rise. She says we now work an extra 164 hours—one full month—each year. She also notes the rise in the two-income household in the last twenty-five years. While we're putting in those longer hours on the job, there's no one at home to clean and cook and plan a social life.

The average American works two months a year more than most Europeans, she adds. Four weeks of time-off a year are mandated by law in Switzerland and Greece, for example, and workers in France and Spain must have *five* weeks. Actual vacation time is often a lot longer (five to eight weeks a year in Sweden).

A recent study by the National Sleep Foundation shows that 38 percent of all full-time workers spend fifty or more hours on the job each week. Investment bankers, medical residents, corporate lawyers, and many other professionals are subject to elastic hours, working more than seventy per week, not including the paperwork they bring home.

HOW WE'RE REALLY SPENDING OUR TIME

Our government agrees that we're working more. A report published in 2004 by the National Institute for Occupational Safety and

Health, Department of Health and Human Services, found that "The average number of hours worked annually by workers in the United States has increased steadily over the past several decades and currently surpasses that of Japan and most of Western Europe."

Surprisingly, a study by Dr. John Robinson, director of the Americans' Use of Time Project at the University of Maryland, and Dr. Geoffrey Godbey, professor of leisure studies in Penn State's College of Health and Human Development, indicates that our free time is increasing as well. Their research, published in the 1999 edition of *Time for Life: The Surprising Ways Americans Use Their Time,* show that we have experienced a steady increase in *free time* over the thirty-five years of the study. Americans between the ages of eighteen and sixty-one years report having forty-one hours a week of free time compared with twenty-five hours a week in 1965. There was a significant gender gap in free time reported with men logging 43.6 hours a week versus 38.5 hours for women. That difference is due largely to the increased number of women working more than twenty hours a week who also spend a significant amount of time performing household chores.

So, we're not only working more, but we have more free time as well.

SUPER-SIZE MY DAY

How can we have more leisure time and work longer hours simultaneously? And why do we still feel rushed? Watching television eats up almost half the average American's free time, Robinson and Godbey report. Perhaps time spent passively absorbing those flickering images somehow doesn't register as "leisure," and we subconsciously subtract it from free time, the time we feel we can choose to spend as we wish.

As a nation, we spend significantly less time in food preparation and household chores than we did in the past. We also spend less time shopping for goods and services. These two findings were reported in a 2006 Federal Reserve Bank of Boston Working Paper, *Measuring Trends in Leisure: The Allocation of Time over Five Decades* by Mark Aguiar and Erik Hurst.

We also spend less time on personal care than we did, which may be a byproduct of the "dress down" and "casual Friday" movements that gained steam in the past decade. The time gained from avoidance of these activities appears to have been banked in the leisure time category.

Yet, most Americans still feel rushed and stressed.

A Pew Research Center report released in 2006 indicated that 23 percent of Americans always feel rushed and another 53 percent sometimes feel rushed. If we look at women alone, 26 percent always feel rushed and 54 percent sometimes feel rushed. It's not surprising that the numbers are even higher for working women with children. A whopping 41 percent of that group report always feeling rushed, and on the other end of the scale, only 7 percent indicated that they never felt rushed. It turns out that working mothers feel they're too busy because they *are* too busy.

Although these figures fluctuate somewhat over time, approximately three-quarters of Americans feel rushed, and we may assume stressed, at least some of the time.

Our jobs create stress and probably always will: there is more to do than time in which to do it even though we're working longer hours; our supervisors are stressed and pass down their stress; industries continue to be in flux as mergers and acquisitions remain commonplace; and positions are unstable as businesses adjust to changing market conditions and increased foreign competition. No surprise that these conditions cause heartburn on a daily basis. Is our free time a source of stress also?

Do we spend half our free time in front of the television because we're too tired to think of anything else to do and even if we could, too tired to do it? Do we have so much to do that the necessity to schedule free time disrupts our enjoyment of leisure activities and saps any rejuvenating qualities they might provide? Definite possibilities. It's also possible that more and more of us are just unable to relax. We carry over our multitasking work habits to our personal lives and try to cram more into each free hour. We use the computer while we're watching television, talk on the phone while shopping, check e-mail on vacation. There is no down time, no time out.

LOGGING YOUR TIME

This book is about you. So how about it? Are you too busy? Are you wasting too much time? No survey or study of the average American's lifestyle will answer that question for you. You get to decide what's a waste of your time. And you get to decide how you're going to spend that time.

First you need to know how you're spending your time now. Are you willing to take a close, honest look at the way you spend your time (which is to say, the way you live)? If you don't like what you find, will you use the results to redirect your efforts and energies?

To do so takes effort and self-awareness. It also takes courage.

Get yourself a notebook to begin this weeklong time logging exercise. Make sure it's portable, able to fit in your purse, coat pocket, backpack, or briefcase. You'll want to have it with you all the time. On the first page of that notebook, list the major categories you want to track. Your list will be different from mine or anybody else's.

Certainly we'll all include the same basic categories, such as "sleep." But you may want to differentiate between "bed sleep" and "nap-in-the-living-room-recliner sleep," for example. This part of the exercise can be very illuminating, as the numbers you gather here may confirm why your spouse keeps telling you to "come to bed."

We'll all have "eat" on our lists of basic time-consuming activities, but again, you may want to split food time into regular sit-down meals, eat-and-run drive-through raids on nutrition, and foraging (or snacking or noshing or whatever you call it).

Is "work" specific enough for you? It depends on how much you want to learn from this self-study. I suspect most of us will want to keep closer tabs on exactly what we're doing at work, breaking time into categories such as "meetings" (perhaps also differentiating between "productive meetings" and "total-waste-of-time meetings"?), "report writing," "responding to telephone inquiries," "commute time" (*Don't* forget commute time, which may be a major and previously unnoted time-consumer), and even "break time." (Don't be afraid to chart breaks. You may well discover that you take too few rather than too many.)

The more categories you create, the more precise and helpful the information, and the more annoying keeping track will be. The more you decide to put in, the more you'll get out later, so err on the side of overscrupulous data-keeping. The information you collect here is going to serve you well.

Let your time log sit overnight and take another look at it, adding and deleting as you see fit. Have you forgotten anything? You can, of course, add items during your survey week if you haven't anticipated everything here. The key is to note the items you're interested in tracking and to be sure your system enables you to account for your time fairly accurately. (It will do no good to list two hours a day as "miscellaneous.")

You're almost ready to start your self-study. First, write down your estimate of how much time per week you spend in each category. You can do this in total hours, in percentage of time spent, or both. When you're done, you'll probably want to convert hours into percentages anyway.

For example, if you figure you average seven hours of sleep a night, you can write "49" (7×7) next to that category on your list. Since there are 168 hours in a week, 49 divided by 168 is 29 percent (actually, 29.167 percent, if you need to be that precise. On the other hand, "about 30 percent" may suit your purpose).

Next to your estimate, write the number of hours/percentage you think you *ought* to be sleeping each week. If in your heart of hearts you believe that Mom was right and that you really do need eight hours of sleep, you'd write in "56/33.3 percent" next to your "49/29 percent."

Now keep your time log for a full week. Try to pick a "typical" week (if there is such a thing) that's neither spent on vacation nor a business trip, and relatively free of major crises. If a crisis does erupt during the week you've chosen, you can always start over the following week.

It is important that you be persistent and precise.

Can you do two activities at once? Of course. In fact, traditional time management books insist you do two, three, even four things at a time. But for the purpose of this survey you're going to decide on the dominant activity at any given time. For example, if you're listening to an audiobook while driving to work your dominant activity is "driving to work." The book-listening is incidental. If you're reading a book with the television on, you need to decide whether you're mostly reading a book or watching television.

Start your log when you wake up on Day One.

6:15 A.M. Lay in bed, semiconscious, "listening" to "Morning Edition."

Make your next notation when you significantly change your activity.

6:32 A.M. Dragged carcass out of bed. Bathroom. Shower. Dress.
6:58 A.M. Breakfast.

The smaller the increments, the more precise the results (and the more work the gathering).

6:59 A.M. Worked sudoku puzzle.
7:02 A.M. Stopped working sudoku puzzle to let dog out in backyard.
7:02:15 A.M. Resumed working sudoku puzzle.

Too precise? I doubt you'd find this level of precision desirable or helpful. I also doubt you'd keep recording that way for a full week. Make your notes in a way that will tell you what you want and need to know about yourself at the end of the week.

Be honest, even if it hurts. Folks tend to fudge downward on time spent playing computer games and upward on time spent exercising, for example. You want a true picture of your activities in a typical week. Then you can decide if you want to change anything.

It can be difficult, but try not to let the process of keeping track of time alter the way you actually spend that time. If you know you're going to have to record it, you may be less likely to want to flop down and watch a *CSI* rerun. But if that's what you would have done without the log, that's what you ought to do with it.

Nobody has to see your log, and you have the power to change anything you don't like about the way you live (and to decide to embrace anything you do—public opinion, spouses excepted, be damned).

Allow enough time at the end of your survey week to do the math. (No, you don't have to note this time on your log. You're finished with that.) Go back to your first page, where you made your list and created your Estimate column and your Ideal column, and write in the Actual numbers. Each entry should now have three sets of numbers after it.

	ESTIMATE	IDEAL	ACTUAL
Sleep	49 (29%)	56 (33.3%)	52 (31%)

If you've been rigorous and honest, you may get some surprises:

	ESTIMATE	IDEAL	ACTUAL
Video gaming	7 (4.2%)	3.5 (2.1%)	42 (25%)

Okay. You're not likely to get that big a surprise. But you may note some relatively large discrepancies among estimates, ideals, and actuals. If so, rejoice. You're a perfect candidate for time management. You may find that by adjusting actual times to conform more closely to your ideal, you'll improve your life significantly.

You may also find that you need to rethink some of your ideal times and your reasons for having established them.

If an adjustment leaps out at you now, note it in a fourth column, "New Ideal," or "Time Management Goal":

	ESTIMATE	IDEAL	ACTUAL	NEW IDEAL
Video gaming	7 (4.2%)	3.5 (2.1%)	42 (25%)	10.5 (6.3%)

Then write the adjustment you intend to make in the form of a declaration:

"I will play video games no more than one and a half hours a day," or

"I will average no more than 10 and a half hours gaming each week."

Congratulations. You've taken the first big step in successful time management. You've accounted for your time. You've perhaps uncovered areas where you may be spending too much of that time and areas where you aren't spending enough. And you've made some initial declarations concerning your future activities. If you did nothing else, this new level of self-awareness and resolve would be extremely helpful to you.

But there's much more you can do, if you're willing, to help yourself spend time wisely and well; not to satisfy the numbers on the chart, but to create a joy-filled as well as productive life.

CHAPTER 3

Busy or Productive?

In the previous chapter you were asked to log how you spent your time during a typical week. Diligence in completing this exercise should provide an accurate and graphic picture of broad categories of time use, a study that you can use to make general decisions about which activities deserve more attention and which deserve less. For example, it should be fairly obvious if you are getting less sleep than you should, or if television watching is eating up more time than you had supposed.

But what if your activities seem balanced, and you still feel the stress of a rushed and unproductive schedule? You are getting about eight hours of sleep most nights, harmonizing hours at work with hours at play, devoting a worthwhile chunk of time to family and friends, spending time exercising and eating healthy, doing everything "right"—but for all your effort, you don't seem to accomplish what you set out to do. You make your list and check off item after item, but still have more items left undone at the end of the day. Are you spending your time working but not achieving, busy but not productive? Could you be working on the "wrong" things and avoiding the most important?

THE NEED FOR BUSYWORK

Rarely is busywork (tasks which are time consuming but of limited value) listed on an employee's job description or considered during a performance review. It is however, an activity engaged in by many individuals as a replacement for more important, meaningful tasks. Why? It's comforting to be busy and therefore unable to take on additional or alternative duties. It allows one to ignore without guilt the needs of colleagues, and resist without fear of reprisal the requests of supervisors. Other tasks may be more difficult or demanding, require interaction with strangers or other unpleasant individuals, involve activities that are unfamiliar and awkward, or have an uncertain outcome. Busywork, by contrast, offers many of the benefits of valuable work without the nasty side effects.

> *"Those who have least to do are generally the most busy people in the world."*
> —Samuel Richardson (1689–1761), British novelist

Most workers believe that it's important to look busy to their bosses, and far too many bosses feel comforted when their direct reports appear as if they're working hard. No one wants to be thought of as a "slacker" by her colleagues, either.

Being engaged in busywork allows us to feel productive without the fear and uncertainty created by changes in duties. By looking busy, we may fool others as well as ourselves, because many people mistake activity for productivity. It would be possible to put a bunch of busywork tasks on your to-do list, use the time-saving techniques in this book, and accomplish your tasks in record time. But, will you have moved forward, accomplished your *real* duties, and reduced your feelings of stress? No. In too many cases then, "busy" is an unacceptable substitute for "productive."

Some observers have suggested that busywork is a creation by upper management made necessary by modern business organization structure to occupy middle managers. This idea has been around for some time.

In this view, middle managers must keep busy when they are not performing their primary duty, which is to monitor the activities of the lower-level production laborers who do the actual work. Fluctuations in workload create soft periods during which obstacles to discontent must be placed in the managers' way. Reports are created, plans are developed, systems are optimized, and meaningless projects completed so that middle managers are kept busy and the basic organizational hierarchy does not collapse.

A molehill man is a pseudo-busy executive who comes to work at 9 a.m. and finds a molehill on his desk. He has until 5 p.m. to make this molehill into a mountain. An accomplished molehill man will often have his mountain finished before lunch.
—Fred Allen (1894–1957), U.S. radio comic

This rather cynical and conspiratorial viewpoint of the contemporary corporation does not reflect modern business management practices. However, it does appear to be reinforced by the frequency with which large corporations, in an effort to reduce expenses and improve their bottom line, lay off a significant segment of their middle managers and continue to operate, seemingly without interruption. These events makes one wonder what all of those middle managers were accomplishing prior to their layoff if the organizations can get along so successfully (better, according to their press releases) after such drastic downsizing.

Whether busywork is an operational tool created by upper management to help maintain the pyramidal organization structure, or a device employed by the individual to avoid other more important tasks, it reduces productivity in direct proportion to the time it consumes. Unfortunately, while busywork may act as a temporary substitute for higher value or necessary work, it does not replace it. Those other tasks will still be there, waiting, and probably becoming more imperative and more complicated as time passes. Concentrating on tasks of limited value can be a real threat to our efforts to manage time by preventing us from working on more important tasks. Yet we feel busy. We feel the stress and pressure of attempting to fit all of our busywork tasks into their allotted time slots, but don't have the sense of accomplishment that would result from completing essential duties.

ARE YOU GUILTY?

How can you recognize if you are involved in work that has little effect on achieving your or your organization's goals? What if your supervisor has assigned you a task or project that you believe to be of little value? Is it still busywork if it's a requirement?

Let's say that the project your manager assigned to you is busywork in your view. Before you create a scene complete with righteous indignation, let's step back for a minute and look at the situation objectively. You may be in a position to determine the project's value, or you may not have all the facts necessary to judge the big picture. The results of this assignment may be on the critical path of someone in the organization unknown to you. So it may *seem* like busywork, and you can waste a great deal of energy and time fighting it, but the fact of the matter is that it needs to be completed. Make sure you understand what's required (and what's not), only spend as much time on it as necessary, and move on to something else.

In general, busywork, and the negative consequence of busywork, implies a choice. We are guilty of performing busywork if we have chosen to avoid more important, goal-related, and potentially difficult assignments by burning up time on tasks that won't matter when they're completed. Or, if we put more effort into a task than it requires. It's possible to spend a lot of time perfecting the appearance of a report—selecting fonts, laying out pages artistically, using graphics—but if this report is an internal document and the readers will be concerned only with its content, then the effort of page beautification is pointless busywork. You have chosen to spend your time on qualities that have no consequence or relevance to the task.

The definition of busywork, then, involves value, and value is a judgment. It's important who is making the judgment. We have seen that a supervisor's judgment can trump that of her employees when it comes to determining a task's value, and the rational employee accepts that fact. In a lot of cases, though, you get to judge a task's value, determine how much effort to put into it, and reap the appropriate rewards when it's completed. Getting the first step correct, making the right judgment call in determining the value of what we're doing, is critical.

AVOIDING BUSYWORK

If required, most of us can provide justification for what we're doing. Even if those tasks that currently occupy our time are not on a critical path within our most important project, we can find enough reasons for continuing to do them to satisfy ourselves. Usually. After all, we are professionals, and we understand better than anyone else what our jobs require.

However, the key to changing our behavior—to stop spending time on busywork and start spending time on more important tasks—is to recognize our flaws rather than protect them. Our flaws, in this case at least, are the inability to fully understand our goals, translate those goals into tasks, and prioritize those tasks in a logical way to accomplish the goals. This is easy to accept in theory, but much more difficult to execute in practice.

That's because other demands interrupt our schedules and lay waste to our plans. There are telephone calls to return and e-mail messages to deal with, colleagues' requests, and minor or major fires to extinguish depending on what stage our projects are in. We may find ourselves well on the way to accomplishing important work only to be ambushed by minor concerns and insignificant duties, so that at the end of the day, we feel tired but unsatisfied with the previous eight hours of frenzied activity.

If busywork is the problem, then eliminating busywork will make us more productive, correct? Not necessarily. We may be engaged in busywork because we are unable or unwilling to accomplish important tasks. And we may be just as unable to accomplish important tasks, for whatever reason, even without busywork. In that case, busywork is not the problem, but may be the symptom of a different problem.

It's just as true, however, that by continuing to perform limited-value tasks, we are less able to accomplish meaningful duties. As mentioned earlier, first, we need to identify our goals in order to understand and prioritize the tasks that lead to accomplishing those goals. Then we must focus our attention on performing those tasks, rather than others. Simple, right? Of course not! If it was, there wouldn't be so many books and magazine articles and workshops designed to help people who are frustrated because they can't seem to manage their time.

CHAPTER 4

Can You Really Manage Time?

W e define time management as a personal rather than a social issue in our culture. It's your problem if you're stressed out and too busy. Take care of it if you can. Just be sure to pay your bills and show up for work on time.

But let's think on a social level for a moment before we buckle down to the job of changing your life.

As a culture, could we establish a six-hour work day, a thirty-hour work week, and a paid vacation for every worker?

Could we support universal alternative working arrangements such as flex time and job sharing?

Could we acknowledge "workaholism" as a true social disorder instead of a badge of honor?

If not, are we willing to count the actual price we pay as a society for health care along with underemployment and unemployment?

CAN YOU CHANGE?

It's not impossible. In the 1950s we decided counteracting the threat of a Communist takeover was our most important priority, and we completely restructured society to do it. (An important reason President Eisenhower created the interstate highway system, for example, was as a means of evacuating our cities in the event of a nuclear attack.) And in the early 1960s John F. Kennedy pledged that the country would have a man on the moon within the decade, and we did it.

Check out the way social attitudes have changed toward cigarette smoking in the last twenty years. That didn't just happen. People worked hard to change those attitudes.

Huge changes in social awareness and values *are* possible. But for now, work on the one part of society you can change—yourself.

JUST WHAT CAN YOU DO ABOUT THE TIME CRUNCH?

Many of us feel that some or all of our life is out of control. It's so commonplace that the feeling has become a lifestyle, recognized and capitalized on by advertisers. Advertisers sell things by connecting with consumers' feelings and adapting their products and services to accommodate those lifestyles. They aren't saying that we should feel out of control. They're assuming that we do—and offering a partial solution, a time saver, an island of tranquillity in an ocean of chaos, one good product that works the way it should.

It should come as no surprise that the advertising community is on to us; their studies, surveys, and focus groups are continually slicing and dicing our habits and preferences into smaller and more manageable pieces. They know, for example, that in 2005 there were 126 billion "on-the-go eating occasions" in the United States. That's more than one per person per day for every man, woman, and child—a lot of snacking. Energized by this knowledge, food manufacturers are eager to supply the fuel (read: snack food) that feeds our need to indulge and helps keep us on the go. All this convenience adds up to a $63 billion a year business.

The food industry, who perfected the drive-through experience, consequently taught us how to eat while driving, an important multitasking skill in today's world. Most providers of goods and services also design time-saving, convenience qualities into their products and feature these characteristics in marketing efforts. The computer hardware and software industries were built on this premise, and stand as icons for productivity improvement. Yet, the desire to manage time is such a universal imperative that it continues to spawn easy-care clothing, labor-saving appliances, electronic toll lanes, and shortcut products for every aspect of our lives. Our cars can park themselves, we can pay for someone to stand in line for us, and can use a cell phone to find the nearest restroom in a strange city, thereby improving our way of life.

Some of these products serve to separate us from our environment and eliminate the need for social intercourse—and we feel that these are additional benefits. Where the woodsman of yore needed a trusty knife for dealing with his environment, we need a raft of tools to prepare us instantly for work and life and to immediately find answers to any questions we may have. When we're too busy, we buy our way out with a product or service to help get us through physically and psychologically.

But here again, we should tally the true price for such conveniences, in time and money spent shopping, in increasing dependence, and in the missed pleasures of cooking and smelling and savoring (and, in many cases, *chewing*) food. We have to count up the toll—on our eyes and stomachs and psyches—when we push ourselves to work ever harder, ever faster, ever longer.

When you start keeping score right, sometimes you'll also start changing some of the decisions you make.

LIMITS TO THE TRADITIONAL TIME MANAGEMENT APPROACH

"You can gain extra minutes and even hours every day by following these tips from a time management expert," the article in the tabloid newspaper announces. (You know the kind of paper I'm talking about, the kind nobody reads, let alone buys, but that somehow boasts a paid circulation in the millions.)

Among these tips from the expert, Lucy Hedrick, author of *365 Ways to Save Time*, is:

- "If you don't have time for reading, letter-writing, cooking or exercise, get up earlier in the morning."

This seems to be a favorite time-management solution. Other experts, the ones who study sleep, estimate that Americans are now getting sixty to ninety minutes less sleep each night than they did ten to fifteen years ago. Not only does she advise less sleep, she also thinks you should . . .

- "Keep your breakfast fast and simple. Try a 'blender breakfast' consisting of a banana, fruit juice, granola and a dash of honey." And,
- "If your bathtub needs a cleaning, do it during your shower. You can scrub as you finish washing or while your hair conditioner is working."

You *could* do those things. You could make up a huge pitcher of "blender breakfast" and keep it in a cooler in your car, so you could drink it on the way to work.

You could take a waterproof CD player into the shower, so you could listen to a self-help program while you're going at the grout with your toothbrush and rinsing the shampoo out of your hair. You could even wear your clothes into the shower, like the protagonist in Anne Tyler's novel, *The Accidental Tourist*, so you could wash your duds while you showered, grouted, and listened.

These techniques might work wonderfully for some folks, but others would pay too high a price for the saved seconds.

You may need to chew your breakfast, so you know you've really eaten; you'll have to live with the inconvenience and the irrevocable passage of time while you chomp your Grape Nuts.

You may want and need the three-minute oasis of a steaming hot shower, a little morning miracle, a pleasure for body and soul, to start even the busiest day.

Some, however, get up early and exercise for forty-five minutes to ninety minutes every morning before chewing their way through breakfast and wallowing in that hot shower. That works for them. It might not work for you.

Some of us listen to music when we jog, and others prefer letting their minds drift. If you were so inclined to make the most of your run, you could install a speakerphone to your treadmill so you could exercise both mind and body simultaneously, and enjoy a glorious multitasking moment.

Some of you need to impose strict order on your work space—a place for everything and everything in its place, with neat files, a clean desktop, a floor you can actually walk on. Others are in the compost heap school of desktop management, and don't mind hurdling the piles of files and books and periodicals that inevitably collect on the floor.

I even found support for the slovenly workplace. In *How to Put More Time in Your Life*, Dru Scott extols "the secret pleasures" of clutter, calling messy folks "divergent thinkers" (which, you have to admit, sounds much better than "messy slob").

The point is—the classic rules of time management don't work for everyone. You have to find your own way through the suggestions and exercises that follow. You may not be able to control some elements of your life, and you may not want to.

There are lots of things none of us can control, like traffic. If you drive a car anywhere more populous than the outback of Australia, you're going to get stuck in traffic. Manage the flow of traffic? You might as well try to manage the current of the river in which you swim.

If you make an appointment, somebody's going to keep you waiting. A phone solicitor will interrupt your dinner. Your boss will dump a last-minute assignment on you. Your child will get sick the same day you have to make that mega-presentation before the board. It happens. The only thing you can do is anticipate and adjust.

SO THAT'S WHERE THE TIME REALLY GOES!

Efficiency expert Michael Fortino offers the following dismal scenario for the average life lived in these United States. In your lifetime you will spend:

seven years in the bathroom,
six years eating,

five years waiting in line,
three years in meetings,
two years playing telephone tag,
eight months opening junk mail, and
six months sitting at red lights.

And on an average day, you'll get interrupted seventy-three times a day(!), take an hour of work home, read less than five minutes, talk to your spouse for four minutes, exercise less than three minutes, and play with your kid for two minutes.

Nightmarish. Want to change that picture? Just as with poor Scrooge, scared into life change by the ghosts of Christmas past, present, and future, it's not too late for you to refocus your life. That's what time management is really all about.

But no matter what you do, you're still going to spend a lot of time idling at red lights, cooling your heels in waiting rooms, and standing in line.

SOME INITIAL CHANGES TO GET CONTROL OF YOUR TIME

You could make large-scale changes. You could quit your job, leave your family, move to a cabin in the Dakotas and paint landscapes. You could. But you probably won't and probably shouldn't.

You can make tiny changes, without needing anybody's help or permission. You can, for example, learn to take four mini-breaks a day, or adopt any of the other tips, as I'll suggest in a later chapter.

As you work your way through this book, let yourself explore as many possibilities as you can. Some won't be practical. Some won't work for you. Some will be beyond your means, for a variety of reasons. But by applying your creativity, initiative, and energy to this exploration, you will find ways to create meaningful, life-affirming change.

CHAPTER 5

Use the To-Do List Effectively

There's nothing new about the to-do list. Folks have been jotting down lists of things they need to do and then checking each item off the list as they do them for a very long time. The more you need to do, and the more pressure you feel to do it, the more helpful the list can be.

Alan Lakein spelled out the uses and misuses of the to-do list in his groundbreaking 1973 book, *Time Management: How to Get Control of Your Time and Your Life.* He showed us how to prioritize those to-do items, making sure we tackled the essential items first. Lakein's idea was to use the list to get everything done, starting with the important. But the overall goal was to live a happy, healthy, well-rounded life. Thankfully for us, Lakein had the wisdom to consider rest, recreation, and relationships as important components of the full life.

Other time management coaches take the tack that more and better organization leads to greater productivity, which is our true goal. David Allen's *Getting Things Done: The Art of Stress-Free Productivity* offers a complete system for capturing and dealing with every task in a straightforward, prioritized manner allowing us to eliminate clutter and stay focused.

Time management consultant Anne McGee-Cooper points out the dangers of too much focus in her book *Time Management for Unmanageable People: The Guilt-Free Way to Organize, Energize and Maximize Your Life.* When you try to get more done in the same amount of time, she counsels, you run the risk of overload, a phenomenon known in computer lingo as "thrashing," when the computer gets too many commands at once and gets stuck trying to decide what to do first.

There are other dangers inherent in developing a list of tasks the night before or during the morning of each workday. To illustrate those dangers, let's look at a sample to-do list, one that makes just about every possible mistake. Here, then, is:

THE TO-DO LIST FROM HELL

We'll impose a mid-level of organization, less than a minute-by-minute script but more than a simple list of tasks.

To do before work
Exercise: 100 situps, 50 pushups, 25 squats
Review agenda and materials for staff meeting
Read *The Wall Street Journal*
Morning commute (17 minutes)
Listen to motivational self-help CD on time management
Morning
Answer faxes, overnight mail, voice mail, e-mail (8 a.m.–9 a.m.)
Staff meeting (9 a.m.–10:30 a.m.)
Organize research for quarterly report (10:30 a.m.–11:45 a.m.)
Drive to lunch meeting (15 minutes)
Lunch meeting (noon–1:30 p.m.)
Afternoon
Write draft of quarterly report (1:45 p.m.–3:00 p.m.)
Meet with committee on workplace expectations (3 p.m.–4:30 p.m.)
Afternoon commute (18 minutes—pick up dry-cleaning)

That's it. There's your workday, all laid out.
Do all that and you'll likely be laid out, too.
Notice that your ability to accomplish all the tasks on your list depends on split-second timing. Everything must go perfectly—no traffic jams, no emergencies, no interruptions.
When's the last time you had a perfect day—no traffic jams, no emergencies, and no interruptions?

That's what I thought.

THE DAY AS YOU REALLY LIVE IT

You sleep through the snooze alarm twice. (You're exhausted from your wrestling match with yesterday's to-do list.) No time for exercise or, for that matter, breakfast—which didn't even make it onto the original list. You're down two, feeling guilty and grouchy before you've even gotten started.

You glance at your meeting notes, skim the left-hand column on the front page of the *Journal,* and sprint to the car. You're in luck. The car starts, even though you've put off getting it serviced—no time. No idiot ruins your day by getting into an accident ahead of you, and traffic flows fairly smoothly.

Even so, the commute takes 18.5 minutes, so you're already running ninety seconds behind. You didn't get to listen to your motivational CD, either, because the CD player in the car jammed. (Better put "get CD player fixed" on your future to-do list.)

You can anticipate the rest. (You don't have to anticipate it. You've *lived* it.) You don't even get close to going through all the voice mail, let alone the e-mail. The meeting starts late and runs long—don't they always? It's too late to tackle the quarterly report, and you spend the rest of the morning answering the phone and battling e-mail.

After a lunch you didn't taste and a meeting you didn't need, you finally get a few minutes for those notes for the quarterly report. You're tired, grouchy, full of a chicken enchilada that refuses to settle down and let itself be digested, and preoccupied with the meeting you've got to get to in a few minutes. No wonder the report refuses to organize itself.

Another meeting (starts late, runs long), another snarling, gut-wrenching commute, a wasted stop at the dry-cleaners (in your rush this morning, you left your claim ticket on the bureau).

Another day shot.

And now it's time to start the second shift, the workday put in at home sweet home.

Pretty dismal scene, isn't it? And not really that much of an exaggeration.

Did the to-do list help? Sure. It provided a record of what you *didn't* get done while you were doing other things, and it helped you to go to bed guilty and frustrated by every unchecked item.

What went wrong? You failed to plan for the unplanned. You weren't realistic about your own capacities or about the real time required to do things. You left important stuff off the list that needed to be done, and spent too much time on low-value busywork.

In short, this wasn't a to-do list. It was a wish list, a fantasy, an unattainable dream, an invitation to frustration and fatigue.

SUGGESTIONS FOR CREATING A HEALTHY TO-DO LIST

The following list of suggestions incorporates some effective techniques for creating an effective to-do list. If some of the suggestions seem to contradict others, it's because they do. It is hoped that some techniques will appeal to certain readers. Embrace those that work for you.

1. Don't Put Too Much on It

This is fundamental. Master this one, and everything else falls into place.

Be realistic in your expectations and your time estimates. Make a real-world list, not an itinerary for fantasyland. Otherwise, you'll spend the day running late, running scared, and just flat-out running to catch up. You won't even have time to notice how your efficiency drops as you become cranky and exhausted.

Think about what absolutely needs your attention, tasks that no one else can do, and put those things on your list. Because you've planned your big projects, calculated how much time they require, and when each stage needs to be completed (haven't you?), put the must-do steps on your list.

But don't jam the list. By putting the absolutely most important, must-do items on your list, you'll find that there is no room for the less important, optional, and even forgettable tasks. That's okay. Let the list help you organize, keep on task, and get the important jobs done.

If by some miracle things take less time than you had allowed for, rejoice! You've given yourself the gift of found time, yours to spend however you want and need to.

To help follow rule #1, follow #2.

2. Put Some Air in It

Overestimate the commute time. Figure in the wait before the meeting, the time spent on hold, the traffic backup. Due to Murphy's Law, planning for a possible traffic jam ensures that it won't occur, and you will arrive early at your destination. Allowing yourself just enough time for your trip, however, guarantees a delay. Now you know.

3. List Possibilities, Not Imperatives

This speaks more to your frame of mind when you make the list than to the specific notations on that list. You're listing those tasks that you hope, want, and, yes, need to finish during the day. You're not creating a blueprint for the rest of the universe, and your plans don't have the force of natural law.

What happens if you don't get to everything on your list? What happens, for example, if you wake up simply too ill to crawl out of bed, let alone tackle the crammed workday?

I'm talking serious sick here, not the borderline sore throat and headache that might keep you in bed on a Saturday but not on a workday. In a way, the serious sickness is easier, because you don't have to decide whether or not to attempt to go to work, and you don't have to feel guilty about staying in bed while the rest of the world is tending to business. (Depending on your tolerance for pain and your level of guilt, you might have to be near death to achieve this state.)

Let's suppose you're sick enough to have to stay flat on your back in bed for two days, and you can barely wobble around the house in bathrobe and slippers on the third. In all, you miss an entire week of work.

Meanwhile, what happened to the stuff on your to-do list?

The meetings went on without you. Folks figured out they could live without the quarterly report for another week. You've got 138 messages on voice mail (sixty-two of them from the same person), 178 e-mails (fifty-two of them copies of replies and replies to replies by multiple recipients on a single question), and a desk awash in memos, faxes, mail, and other unnatural disasters. You take stuff home for a week, trying to get caught up.

That's bad, but it isn't *that* bad. You didn't die. You didn't lose a loved one. Western civilization did not grind to a halt. Commerce and government managed to struggle on without you.

It's too late to respond to some of those urgent e-mails and messages, but it turns out they really didn't need a response after all.

Try to remember that the next time you're relatively healthy but nevertheless falling behind on the day's tasks.

Think you've had a bad day at the office? Consider former Los Angeles Dodger center fielder Willie Davis, who met his own personal disaster during the second game of the 1965 World Series against the Baltimore Orioles. In the top of the fifth inning of a 0–0 tie, with Dodger ace Sandy Koufax on the mound, Davis managed to make three errors in one inning, including two on the same play, to blow the game. The Dodgers never recovered, losing the series in four straight games.

After his record-setting game, Davis was philosophical. "It ain't my life," he told a vast radio and television audience. "And it ain't my wife. So why worry?"

Another baseball player/philosopher, Satchel Paige, put it this way: "Don't look back. Something might be gaining on you."

God, give us grace to accept with serenity the things that cannot be changed, courage to change the things which should be changed, and the wisdom to distinguish one from the other.
—Reinhold Niebuhr (1892–1971), U.S. theologian

But we don't really believe or act on such adages.

None of this is to suggest that what you do isn't important—at least as important as playing baseball. I'm simply saying that you, and I, and everybody else, need to keep things in proper perspective.

4. Schedule Your Tasks

If you can assign a time slot in your day to accomplish a particular task, there is a much greater likelihood that you will actually do it. You will be mentally prepared, committed to tackling the job, and less prone to distractions if it's scheduled with a beginning and end point. With onerous tasks in particular, scheduling a one-hour or just a half-hour period makes the job less threatening.

5. Don't Carve the List in Stone

Your list has to be flexible if it's going to do you any good. You have to be able to change it, digress from it, flip it on its ear, add to it, wad it up and toss it in the recycle bin—if it's really going to help.

Find a flexible format that works for you. If you like an intricate grid system, with squares for every five minutes during the day, go for the grid. If you keep your list on a PDA, complete with abbreviations that only you understand, that's fine. If crayon on butcher paper is more your style, start scrawling.

Don't try to fit a format; none are perfect. Try some or all of them until you find or create a format that works for you.

6. Order Creatively

Make sure the most important tasks get done before you drown in a sea of relative trivia. Answer the e-mail first if it's absolutely the top priority on your list. If it isn't, schedule it for later in the day, or if possible, establish one or two periods at the same time every day to tackle e-mail. Don't do it first simply because it's there, demanding attention, or because it's relatively easy, or because you've gotten into the habit of doing it first. It's too easy to be caught up in an extensive e-mail conversation on a marginal project, and find that half of your morning is shot.

Try to vary your pace, alternating difficult and easy, long and short, jobs requiring creative thought with rote functions. Change activities often enough to keep fresh.

Attack mentally taxing jobs when you're most alert and energetic. For most of us, this means first thing in the morning. If you save them for later, you're admitting that you aren't going to work on them.

7. Turn the Big Jobs into Small Jobs

When large tasks are involved, it's important to define and isolate (divide and conquer) the components of the task. In fact, it's essential to break down a large task into small tasks to understand what steps are involved and in what order they must be completed in order to finish the larger goal.

If one of your tasks is writing a product development plan, for example, and you know the amount of time and effort it will consume, defining the parts of the plan will make it much more controllable. You may avoid the task if it's "write a product development plan," but "collect competitive data" is much more approachable. By allotting just half an hour to this step, you're more likely to do it and reap that sense of accomplishment towards the overall goal.

8. Schedule Breaks, Time-Out Time, and Little Rewards

Most of us schedule "rest" for last—if we schedule it at all. By the time we get to it, *if* we get to it, it's too late to do us any good.

If you don't put rest on the list, you won't do it. So put it on the list with a start point and an end point. And don't save it for last. Plan the rest for when it will do you some good, before you become too tense or exhausted. Brief rests at the right times will help you maintain a steady, efficient work pace.

Instead of waiting until the end of the day for that 15 minutes of pleasure reading, for example, schedule three five-minute reading breaks during the day. You may even want and need to schedule that game of catch with your kid or that walk around the neighborhood with your spouse. You can even use software that will alert you to your scheduled breaks so you don't have to remember them.

A word of semi-serious caution here, which is best stated by Glasser's Corollary of Murphy's Law:

> *If, of the seven hours you spend at work, six hours and fifty-five minutes are spent working at your desk, and the rest of the time you throw the bull with your cubicle-mate, the time at*

which your supervisor will walk in and ask what you're doing can be determined to within five minutes.

9. Schedule Long-Range Personal Goals

You know you should do some serious financial planning. You know you should have a current will. You know you should create a systematic plan for home maintenance and repair.

If you know all that and never seem to get to it—put it on the schedule. And, again, if you schedule these goals in manageable steps, you'll be much more likely to actually do them.

10. Be Ready to Abandon the List

"If you only write the story that is planned," writer and teacher Ellen Hunnicutt tells her students, "you miss the story that is revealed."

The same goes for the story of your life. The most important thing you do all day, all year, or even all lifetime, may never appear on any to-do list or show up on the day planner. Never get so well organized and so scheduled that you stop being alert to life's possibilities—the chance encounter, the sudden inspiration.

Not all surprises are bad surprises. It just seems that way sometimes.

For a delightful depiction of the dangers of developing list addiction (which surely must have its own twelve-step programs and support groups by now), read "A List," one of Arthur Loebel's delightful Frog and Toad stories for children.

"I have many things to do," Toad realizes one morning. "I will write them all down on a list so that I can remember them."

He writes down "wake up" and, realizing that he's already done that, crosses it off—a great momentum-builder.

Other items include "getting dressed," "eating breakfast," and "going for a walk with Frog."

Disaster strikes when a gust of wind snatches the paper from Toad's hand and poor Toad finds himself incapable of acting without the list to guide him.

Toad's story has a happy ending. You'll just have to make the time to read it for yourself.

11. You Don't Have to Make a List

The to-do list is a tool. Techniques for creating an effective list are suggestions, not commandments. If they help, follow them— adapting and modifying to fit your own circumstances and inclinations. If they don't help, make your own kind of list, or don't make any list at all. If you find yourself spending too much time making and revising the list, for example, or if you never refer to the list once it's completed, then the to-do list may not be for you. You won't have "failed time management." You'll have simply investigated a process that helps some folks and not others, and found that you are in the "not others" category.

Bonus Suggestion: Create a Not-to-Do List

Along with noting and organizing the tasks you'll do, you might also want to write down those things you *won't* do.

I'm not talking about the sorts of epic life-pledges that appear on lists of New Year's resolutions, stuff like: stop smoking, don't nag, and cut consumption of chocolate. You can certainly make that kind of list if you find it helpful. Instead, I'm referring to day-to-day tasks that have fallen to you by custom, habit, or lot, but that should be done by someone else or not done at all.

Examine large tasks (serving on the school board) and small ones (responding to every memo from the district supervisor) to make sure (1) they need to be done and (2) you're the one who needs to do them. If the task fails on either count, put it on the *not*-to-do list.

Time management isn't just or even primarily about doing more things in the same amount of time or doing the same number of things in less time. Time management involves choosing to do the *right* things.

CHAPTER 6

Get Started

M ost of us suffer to some extent from work-aversion. Some of us like our work, and most of us at least don't hate it, but we'd still rather be doing something else most of the time. That's why they call it "work," right? That aversion makes getting started the hardest part of any job.

JUMP-START EACH WORK SESSION

"Writer's block" gets the most press, but folks encounter "executive's block" and "plumber's block" and "computer programmer's block," too—that state of semiparalysis brought on by fear and pain and just plain old lack of desire.

We all have to learn to work through the aversion if we want to put food on the table. But some of us perform time-consuming warmup rituals before we start to work, and many of us take far too long to reach a productive level of activity.

You may not even be aware of your rituals, which makes them hard to get rid of. Some of your warmups may actually help prepare you to work, but others may simply postpone the inevitable confrontation. Those are a waste of time, and you need to get rid of them. Here's how.

EIGHT WAYS TO GET A FAST START

1. Prepare Mentally

Back at the turn of the century, a man named Charles Haanel called the subconscious mind "a benevolent stranger, working on your behalf." For all our subsequent research on the working of the brain, that remains a perceptive description.

You can get that subconscious stranger working for you on any job you have to perform.

The night before the job, settle in your mind exactly what you want to accomplish the following day. You're not issuing orders here. You're not telling the subconscious how you intend to do the job. That's part of the conscious planning stage.

You're simply planting the idea, giving that larger mind that exists outside of conscious thought time to mull and sift, combining images and ideas, amassing energy and positive attitude.

Instead of letting the subconscious disaster tapes play, visualize yourself performing exactly as you wish. This is particularly helpful if you're going to speak to a group or otherwise put yourself before an audience.

This isn't a matter of "wishing will make it so." Positive visualization won't cast a magic spell over your audiences. But it will affect *your* behavior, helping you call forth your best effort by concentrating energies and consciousness. This preparation will give your mind an opportunity to rehearse an event before the fact, and to call forth "memories" when it actually takes place, rather than react with surprise.

For some great athletes, this ability seems to be a natural gift, no less than speed, strength, and coordination. They talk about a strange kind of prescience during which they seem to see themselves hitting the home run, intercepting the pass, or returning the backhand baseline volley before they actually make the play.

What comes to some as a gift you can develop as a tool.

2. Prepare Physically

An obvious step is to have your physical tools assembled and accessible before you begin the job. If possible, stake out a specific place for the work, where you can keep everything you need within easy reach and not have to stow it between work sessions.

That way, you eliminate time spent pitching camp and then tearing it down again each time.

Also, when you become accustomed to doing a job in a specific place, you'll be focused and ready to work as soon as you enter that place. This is another example of mind conditioning; you're training your mind to perform a certain function in a certain place. This place doesn't have to be fancy or even private. It just has to be yours, and it has to have the tools you need.

3. Map the Terrain

Before you begin the trip, figure out exactly where you want to go, and what the destination looks like. This is another basic requirement in order to reach a successful conclusion, but it's astonishing how often the trigger will be pulled before the gun is properly aimed.

Remind yourself of your purpose. What's in it for you? For your organization? For the client or customer? If you can't answer these questions, save yourself time and effort—and ensure that you'll do a better job—by taking a few moments now to get the information you need and to focus on what you hope to accomplish.

If you still aren't sure, seek out the authorization, approval, or verification you need. Again, a few minutes spent here can save hours later. And you'll work more efficiently and confidently.

If the work involves several stages, write them down first. Don't try to create the sort of orderly outline only an English teacher could love. Just jot down the steps or ideas in the order they occur to you. Then number the items in proper sequence. If it is still difficult to create this simple list of steps, by now you should be alerted to the fact that you have a problem.

4. Start Anywhere

If you aren't ready to start at the beginning, start someplace else.

You can't escape certain sequences. A plumber has to turn off the water before disassembling the pipes, for example. But jobs often contain a great deal of flexibility. The finished product may need to be assembled in the proper order, but you don't necessarily have to tackle the components in that order.

A director shoots a movie in the most practical sequence, getting all the location shots before returning to the studio for the interiors, for example. These separate scenes become the raw material for the finished movie. If the director and the editors do their jobs well, the viewer can't tell (and doesn't care) in what order the scenes were shot; the movie tells a coherent, entertaining story. The seams don't show.

When you're thinking your way through a problem, it doesn't matter where you start. Often, it is more productive to start at the end of the puzzle and work backwards. Just start somewhere.

5. Start Anyway

Lots of writers have suffered from blocks at one time or another. Poets seem especially susceptible to the disease.

But the working stiffs who write on deadline day after day never seem to get blocked.

Lots of times they write when they feel lousy. Lots of times they worry that lack of time has forced them to do a lousy job. Folks who can't afford to get writer's block don't get it.

The same goes for plumber's block, CEO's block, and bus driver's block.

The poet can afford to wait for inspiration. The rest of us do the job, inspired or not.

If you're good at your work, a professional in the best sense of the word (whether or not you're getting paid), your mood doesn't show in the finished product. Nobody can tell whether or not you felt like doing it. In fact, they don't care. They're interested in the results, and the results can be just as good regardless of the mental anguish you felt forcing yourself to complete the task.

6. Lock Out the Critics

We all make mistakes. Some of us get to make ours in private, and we can give ourselves the chance to fix them before anybody else sees them. But when a quarterback throws an interception, every football fan in the stadium sees him do it (and more will see the replay or read about it), and there's no way he can pull the ball back and take the play over. Lots of us work that way also. There's no time for a redo, there's barely enough time to get it done the first time, and we feel the eyes of the boss or customers on us as we work our way through a challenge.

It's a two-step process, first the doing, and then the judgment. Just as an NFL quarterback has to shut out the howling of the mob and concentrate on the receiver, you have to shut out concerns about judgment during the process of creation. If you don't, you won't take a chance, try out an idea, risk a "failure" in the eyes of the invisible judge.

7. A Job Worth Doing

If we look again at the previous two suggestions, we realize that a job worth doing is worth doing—poorly. As difficult as this may seem for people who were taught to be perfect, we must realize at some point that our best intentions, planning, and efforts count for nothing if the job doesn't get done. The unwritten book may be perfect; the product that never makes it to the shelf could be the best and most profitable in your company's history. No one will ever know.

8. Stop Before You Need To

"Don't stop me. I'm on a roll."

Momentum is a wonderful feeling, especially when we've got a lot to do and not much time to do it. An interruption is the last thing you want when the job is going well. Common sense tells you to keep working until you're finished. If you can't finish the job in one sitting, you work until you're exhausted or until you run into a snag you can't work your way through.

But it can make a lot more sense to stop before you get too tired and before you reach a snag.

If you stop because you're stuck, you carry that "stuckness" with you until the next work session. You'll sit back down to the task and immediately be faced with the same problem that stopped you previously. And if you give yourself too much time between work sessions, you'll build up an aversion to the task, the very material blocks are made of.

But if you've stopped in midstride, sure of the next step you'll take, you'll come back to the job confident and even eager. You won't have to waste any time getting back into the groove, because you won't have gotten out of it. This is a technique used by many successful writers, who would have a significant problem starting up if they hadn't stopped while "on a roll."

There is an exception to this "rule" and whether the rule or its exception applies to you depends on the type of person you are, and how you tend to work through problems. Most of us just keep punching until we make a hole in the wall, but some individuals receive problem-solving inspiration while engaged in activities not directly related to the task. I knew one fellow who did his best thinking while running; he'd break from a task when he hit a snag, go for a run, and by the time he returned he typically had found a solution. If your mind works in this nontraditional way—like setting a PC to defrag while you go off and do something else—then don't tamper with your system. Encourage it and use it to your advantage.

Is Your Life a Constant Come-from-Behind Rally?

Time is running out and your team is trailing. Things look bleak; your guys have no chance; there's not enough time left. But the team, made of sterner stuff, reaches down deep, and with an effort suitable for a Hollywood epic, rallies in the final seconds to win. The fans go wild, drowning out the commentator who's screaming hysterically "I can't believe it! I can't believe it!"

It's the most exciting come-from-behind win of the season and an absolute joy to watch, whether it's football, baseball, soccer—any team sport. But as a way of living, the rally has its drawbacks.

You Know You're Running Your Rally When . . .

- You charge from meeting to meeting, appointment to appointment, with no time to gather your thoughts;
- You've taken lunch at your desk so often, your keyboard's clogged with crumbs;
- The ringing phone makes you jump;
- You feel one bad surprise away from throwing up your hands and screaming;
- A longtime friend calls to tell you she's coming to town and would love to see you, but you make excuses because there's just no way you can spare the time;
- You aren't getting any exercise, but you feel exhausted;
- You crawl into bed at last—and can't fall asleep.

We all go through days, even weeks like that. For short spells, it can even be exhilarating—as long as we can keep one jump ahead of disaster. But the longer you sustain this killer pace, the more you suffer and the less efficient you become—not just in your work but in every aspect of life.

CALL A TIME OUT

If you wait for life to ease up and for the bad surprises to stop coming, you may wait too long. You have to call an end to the rally and start working at a more normal pace, for yourself, your loved ones, and your colleagues. But the more you worry about relaxing, the more tense you become. What now?

You need to learn how to slow down the pace, to normalize your efforts so they're consistent and effective rather than enduring a daily train wreck. By relaxing mind and body four or five times a day, you can achieve the control you need to reduce stress and be more productive.

TAKING MINI-VACATIONS EVERY DAY

Take your break before you need it. Don't wait to be exhausted, and don't wait to be stuck. Break your momentum—and the buildup of stress and fatigue—with a sanity break in the midst of the chaos. Make the break a good habit, three or four times a day.

Here are six simple break activities (and an advanced technique for you fast learners). After you read them, jot down three or four more of your own.

SEVEN WAYS TO GO ON VACATION WITHOUT LEAVING YOUR DESK

1. The Breath Break

Here's the simplest, cheapest vacation you'll ever take. For two minutes, just breathe. Take air way down into your belly. You should actually be able to feel your stomach rise with the intake of breath.

But haven't you been breathing already? Sort of. But as you hurry, and as you feel the pressure build inside you, your breath becomes shallow, and you don't get the oxygen you need. You'll especially notice this when you have to speak in front of a group. Your voice rises and gets squeaky, and your throat becomes dry and sore.

To combat the ill effects of this oxygen debt, you don't have to empty your mind or chant a mantra or wrap yourself into a yoga position. All you have to do is breathe deeply and slowly for a couple of minutes three, four, even five times a day. In private, with your feet up and your eyes closed would be nice, of course, but you can take a breath break in the middle of a meeting, behind the wheel of the car, or on the phone. Nobody needs to know you're sneaking oxygen.

2. The Continental Drift

Think of a place of perfect contentment in your life, or hearken back to a time when you were truly relaxed and at peace. (You may have to go all the way back to summer vacation during your elementary school years.) Or create an imaginary oasis.

Then go there for two minutes.

Shut out everything else, close your eyes, and create the scene in your mind. See, hear, feel it. Let warmth and peace wash over you.

You may feel goofy the first few times you try this, but once you've mastered the technique, you'll return refreshed after just a couple of minutes, and you'll know you can go back again soon.

3. Pack Up Your Troubles

Something bothering you? Visualize and get rid of it.

Picture your nemesis, hot branding iron in hand, sneering at you, ready to poke and prod. If your anger and frustration has an abstract source, give it a specific shape. Lack of time making you crazy? Picture a clock gone berserk, its hands spinning out of control. Or make time into a huge *Indiana Jones*–style boulder, rolling toward you with desperate speed.

Then put the image into a bubble and imagine that bubble floating slowly up and away, becoming smaller and smaller until it finally disappears.

Action-movie alternative: Forget the gentle bubble stuff. Blow your troubles to smithereens.

Hey? Are you starting to enjoy this? Good. That's what vacations are for.

4. The Shoulder Shrug

We tend to take out our tensions on specific parts of our bodies. Shoulders are one of my favorite targets. Without knowing I'm doing it, I tense my shoulders as I work. If I don't catch myself, I end up with a sore neck and shoulders and a pounding headache.

I can break the tension, save my shoulders, and avert the headache by remembering to relax my shoulders and rotate them slowly and gently for a couple of minutes. On particularly bad days, the results are dramatic. My shoulders seem to drop several inches, and a soothing warmth flows up my neck.

I never even realize how tense I am until I unclench my muscles and relax. How about you? Are you tensing and clenching while you work?

5. The Phrase for the Day

This one takes a bit of preparation, but it's well worth the effort. Collect pithy bits of wisdom, interesting observations, intriguing fragments of ideas, funny phrases, anything that snags your fancy. You can catch them everywhere—from the media, from conversation, from your own boundlessly creative and endlessly curious mind. Get in the habit of jotting them down as you run across them.

If you find that it's too time consuming to find these phrases on your own, purchase a calendar of daily wisdom or jokes or observations—whatever triggers you most effectively.

When it's time for a break, pull out one of the phrases, read it a couple of times, and let yourself chew on it for two minutes. Don't direct your thoughts. Just let them wander where they will.

6. The Object of Your Affection

Hold a picture of a person you treasure, an object that has special meaning for you, or a talisman (like that lucky silver dollar you've lugged around with you for years). Spend two minutes with it, again letting your thoughts roam.

7. Advance Resting Technique, for the Gifted and Talented

Combine the breathing with any other relaxation activity.

WHY THE TWO-MINUTE BREAK WORKS

Will a two-minute break really do you any good?

Yes. It really will. But you may feel uncomfortable breathing from your tummy the first few times, and you may not notice the effects right away. But if you stick with it, you'll feel the difference.

Here's why.

As you come under fire in the daily wars, your body instinctively reacts, tensing muscles and doling out emergency rations of adrenaline and other natural uppers, getting you ready to fight your enemies or run away from them. These automatic responses will work against you when you've got no one to fight and nowhere to run.

These reactions can build on themselves, and you can get caught in a dangerous loop. You sense danger, and your body responds. That response in turn seems to verify the perception of danger and triggers still more response.

No wonder you can't relax at the end of the day!

But the cycle can work for you as well as against you. If you can relax your body—slowing your breathing, calming your heart—by taking a two-minute break, your panic will subside. You'll regain focus, clarity, and energy.

FREE 21-DAY SATISFACTION-GUARANTEED TENSION TRIAL

I can assure you that these techniques have helped me greatly. You can prove that they work for you by trying them for twenty-one days before drawing any conclusions about their effectiveness. Break up your day with three or four of these short breaks for three weeks and see if you notice the difference.

But I'll warn you right now: you won't remember to rest on your own. You're going to have to build these breaks into your daily routine, and you'll probably even need to plant reminders, in the form of a note in the briefcase, a Post-it on the monitor, a reminder in your computer calendar.

How about it? Are you willing to try? You have nothing to lose but tension and that "quiet desperation" Thoreau warned us about so many years ago.

CHAPTER 8

Get Organized

A report issued by the National Institute for Occupational Safety and Health (NIOSH) in 1999 on stress in the workplace concluded that 40 percent of workers consider their job very or extremely stressful. In another study, the Attitudes in the American Workplace VII survey sponsored by the Marlin Company and conducted by Harris Interactive in 2001, a third of workers said their jobs were harming their physical and emotional health; 42 percent said job pressures were interfering with their personal relationships. In this study, 50 percent of workers claimed they and their fellow workers had a more demanding workload than they had a year ago, and nearly that percentage said they have too much work to do and/or too many unreasonable deadlines. Interestingly, 73 percent said that they would not want their boss's job. A Gallup survey conducted in 2006 confirmed that at least four out of ten Americans who are employed full time or part time say they frequently experience stress. This survey also found that 61 percent of full-time workers say they do not have enough time to do the things they want to do.

Tough and unrelenting workloads, compounded by unexpected demands from other sources, can create a feeling of stress and frustration, negatively impacting our attitude, productivity, and even our health. Clearly, these pressures have an important impact on our lives. If we were better able to manage job and life pressures, we would not feel such stress and be subject to its influence. By using an organizational scheme that captures our personal and work tasks, defines the steps of those tasks, and defines our priorities, we can take much better control of our lives.

RECOGNIZE THE REALITY

We face many tasks, from the small and insignificant (oiling that squeaky hinge on the bathroom door) to the major and consequential (making an important presentation, finding a retirement home for Dad). All of these tasks compete for our attention, and while some may be more significant than others—the health and happiness of Dad should take precedence over a noisy door, after all—they all are part of the nagging "undones" that crowd our conscious and unconscious minds. We can't completely control how our minds work, which accounts for random thoughts and unfortunate sequences, such as remembering to put a stamp on an envelope after mailing it. It also means that we are likely to be thinking about the upcoming presentation during a golf game, and how to correct that nasty slice, in the middle of a staff meeting. Thoughts of squeaky hinges and retirement homes will seem to pop up at inappropriate times as well.

This great mass of random thoughts will keep churning; the pace of life guarantees that more will crowd in before we can deal with the ones already bumping into each other. What to do? Confront the reality that we have many requirements on our time, interruptions are a given, and, unless you're living the rustic life of a reclusive shepherd, that work, family, friends, and community will continue to demand our attention in unplanned ways at inconvenient times. Your son will fall during recess at school breaking his wrist, and will need to be taken to the emergency room, *now*. Your boss will stop by your office and ask you to research a contract and get back to her with the information before lunch. A colleague will call you with "just a couple of questions" and inevitably consume a half hour covering everything from the project status to yesterday's football game.

These are life's side effects. We can't control these events; we only can control ourselves in how we react to them. It's possible to practice techniques to deal with and lessen the effects of interruptions: screening calls and removing the guest chair from your office so visitors can't sit down, for example. Some techniques actually may be worth trying, particularly if you believe you suffer excessively from others' attempts to take advantage of you. But generally, others are just trying to do their jobs, and the evil intent you attribute to them is more revealing of your own insecurity. In the long run, it's more practical to face the interruptions for what they are and deal with them. If we don't react rationally, events can easily overwhelm and prevent us from functioning.

CAPTURE THE TASKS

Having recognized that we probably have more tasks than time in which to do them, and that new demands will arise before we've had a chance to finish the old, we need to apply a control mechanism. Otherwise, current and new tasks will accumulate and become a crushing obstacle to progress. To control our tasks, we first need to capture them in a way that is as easy, fast, and painless as possible. (See Chapter 5, Use the To-Do List Effectively, for another discussion of specific list-making tips.) Many mediums will serve this purpose: sticky notes or index cards (useful for rearranging things if there are many), or a notepad (useful to see the big picture at one glance). Or, you may prefer to do this step in a word processing or spreadsheet file—whatever is the most natural way to capture all responsibilities and uncompleted tasks.

This step is going to seem random in part, because it's essential to capture all tasks, not just the critical ones, but not in any specific order. So, once you've covered all the projects for which you're responsible at work, let the mind wander to extracurricular matters, and try to capture all of your non-work related tasks. Include everything (this step is not an attempt to prioritize, that comes later). To the best of your ability, include personal commitments and all those responsibilities that come with whatever roles you play: spouse or partner, parent, child, sibling, friend, colleague, team member, home owner, volunteer, supporter, advisor, contributor, etc. It is crucial to include the continuing long-term obligations as well as the single near-term tasks. How to capture something as nebulous as

"Spending time with family"? You certainly can capture your son's weekly lacrosse games and your daughter's regular soccer practice. And including an item "Spending time with family" is a good idea, as it will force you to think further and plan how to accomplish this goal. This is a good time to commit to a weekly or biweekly "date" with your spouse or significant other, too.

You may feel that it isn't necessary to include the obvious family responsibilities that come with being a spouse or parent on your list. "I'm doing these things anyway," you reason. Maybe you're the best parent and/or spouse on two legs, and don't wish to cheapen the time you spend with your loved ones by labeling those experiences as "tasks" and scheduling them on the impersonal medium of a task list. Remember that you're building a list of commitments, and creating a device to ensure that these commitments are met.

Collecting this master set of tasks or super "to-do" list, in whatever format you choose, will undoubtedly represent a major effort, but is a step that you may not need to repeat if you maintain the "schedule" part discussed below. Unfortunately, however, the classic to-do list does not permit an understanding of the task, nor does it accommodate a plan or acknowledge what resources, such as time, are necessary to accomplish it. So, at this stage, "Oil the bathroom door" has the same weight as "Write a will." In that regard, your list is as random and disorganized as your unconscious mind. The next steps will address that problem.

DEFINE

Now that you have captured all of your outstanding responsibilities and undone tasks, it's time to define them. This step is essential in being able to prioritize, schedule, and develop a plan to accomplish them. During this stage, you define the steps involved in completing the task and decide how long each will require to complete. The small tasks, such as oiling the hinge on the bathroom door, get a small time window because the task only involves finding the oil and squirting a few drops on the hinge . . . and wiping up the oil that dripped on the floor. If you know where to find the oil and if you don't drip oil on the carpet, the whole project is a five-minute job. Heck, you can do that on the way to dinner, and other than the lack of a squeak, no one will even notice.

If you don't know where the oil is, or if you don't have any oil, or if there's a white carpet under that hinge and you are incorrigibly messy, then the job involves more steps and is going to take much longer. But by going through this definition stage, you can account for all these factors.

For larger tasks, this definition stage is proportionally more important. If your assignment involves other people, getting them to agree, money, contracts, the government, the weather—this list can get fairly long—then the process can approach the complexity of project management. That makes the definition stage crucial for complex tasks as it permits those tasks to be broken down into smaller, more manageable tasks. In fact, it is only by breaking down a large task into small tasks that it's possible to understand what steps are involved and in what order they must be completed. It is in the defining stage that the seemingly impossible and intimidating becomes possible.

If one of your tasks is writing a report, for example, and you are enthusiastically avoiding the project knowing the amount of time and effort it will consume, defining the parts of the report will make it much more controllable. You were probably told in school that writing an outline is the best way to develop a report; it still is an excellent method for organizing your thoughts. Or, you may prefer the mind map method of capturing ideas as described elsewhere in this book. By allotting even half an hour to this organizational step, it will provide a sense of accomplishment towards the overall goal.

PRIORITIZE

Prioritizing is an important part of the organization and control process. Priorities are those activities that influence your ability to reach your goals, so it's necessary to define your goals before you can determine your priorities. Defining your goals will force you to think long term and consider life objectives involving family and friends, community, and self-improvement, as well as work goals.

Because you don't have enough time to complete all of your tasks, prioritizing is essential. Large tasks will require more time to complete, but that does not necessarily mean they should receive priority, or be scheduled in your "prime time." Small tasks can and should be completed quickly, but they should be prioritized using the same rules as the large tasks.

What rules? This is the point where you should look dispassionately at your list of tasks and decide what is most important, which require your attention, and which can be put off. You may be inclined to put out fires first (the urgent tasks), particularly at work, but depending on their importance, some can be left to burn out by themselves. Figure 8.1, a grid made popular by Stephen Covey, may be helpful in forcing you to ask two questions about each task:

IMPORTANT URGENT (A)	IMPORTANT NOT URGENT (B)
NOT IMPORTANT URGENT (C)	NOT IMPORTANT NOT URGENT (D)

Figure 8.1

Ken Blanchard, in his book, *The On-Time, On-Target Manager: How a "Last-Minute Manager" Conquered Procrastination* developed a variation of this grid, shown in Figure 8.2.

HAVE TO DO WANT TO DO (A)	HAVE TO DO DON'T WANT TO DO (B)
DON'T HAVE TO DO WANT TO DO (C)	DON'T HAVE TO DO DON'T WANT TO DO (D)

Figure 8.2

Either of these grids offers an excuseless means of qualifying the nature of a task. You may wish to assign a rating to your tasks; pick a range that's convenient to work with, if you decide to do this. If you use "1" through "10," you can be more precise, but it may not be worth the extra effort in distinguishing between a "6" or a "7" when a simple "A," "B," "C," or "D" will suffice. You'll still end up with a lot of tasks with the highest value in your range, but it's likely that you'll simply discard some as well. You will also find that as you weigh the importance of a task, rereading some old magazine articles, for example, you will change that task to a more practical one, such as "discard old magazines."

SCHEDULE

At this point, your tasks have been captured, defined, and prioritized. You have expended a lot of effort in getting this far in the process, despite the fact that none of your tasks have been completed. There is one more step in managing your tasks that greatly increases the likelihood of their completion: scheduling.

You must assign a place in your schedule for each of your tasks. This scheduling is a commitment to yourself and to others, by showing that you have a plan for each task and have allotted time in which to complete the plan. A to-do list by itself does not accomplish this, and makes your tasks easier to ignore. There are many daily planners suitable for scheduling. When choosing a planner, portability, capacity or space, and editability are important qualities to keep in mind. Because you should use a single planner to schedule all of your duties, it must be convenient to keep with you and transport between locations. You will also want to be thorough in describing each task, so you will need room to write and make notes. And, because the meeting you were planning to prepare for has been postponed for a week, you will need to reschedule the preparation task in your planner with a minimum of effort.

Start with your regular and repeating responsibilities. The meetings you attend every week, the checkups with your reports and your boss, any recurring event should be scheduled (if it's not already). It will be possible to cancel or reschedule a meeting if necessary, but laying them out should prevent most major conflicts. You may not have assigned a high priority score to some of your meetings, feeling that little is accomplished in a particular get-together. However, if you are expected to attend, then it should go into the schedule.

Next, take your highest priority tasks, those you've objectively determined are most important (the "As" and "Bs"), and schedule each one, assigning a fixed slot with beginning and ending times. If you have been thorough in the definition stage, and conscientious in the prioritizing stage, it should be possible to schedule most steps in the largest of projects. If you rely on project management software for scheduling of complex projects, then your personal planner should at least reflect your time commitments, even if the particular task is not specified. It's important to know that certain time slots will not be available for other tasks.

You may be alarmed at this point if your planner is beginning to fill up and you still have many tasks to schedule. You may take comfort in the fact that your tasks are prioritized—it should prepare you for the reality that you have more to do than time permits. It will be difficult for some individuals to realize that they simply cannot accomplish everything they're expected to do. The rational among us will not be surprised, however, but will continue to schedule tasks in the time slots remaining, and when the schedule is full, stop.

Cramming, by the way, is not allowed. During the definition stage, you determined how much time is required to complete each task. If you attempt to cram a two-hour task into a one-hour time slot on your schedule, you will not be able to complete it and will end up rushing the task, cutting corners and quality. You must decide, even before starting, that it needs to be rescheduled to a time when you can dedicate the necessary hours to its completion.

You will find leftover tasks because your schedule is full. Despite their being low priority tasks—if you didn't fill up your schedule only with highest priority tasks—you still need to manage them. Some should be discussed with your boss if they are part of your assigned duties (bring along your planner for this discussion). Others should be negotiated with the appropriate stakeholders—family, friends, committee members. Having your planner during the negotiations and permitting others to see your schedule is worth a few credibility points. Ideally, you will be able to shift responsibility for a low priority task to someone else; if not, move the due date to a time you can accommodate, or reduce your involvement to a manageable level.

You may wish to make your schedule available to others, certainly anyone having responsibility to schedule your time. Technology is on your side if you've chosen a planner that can easily synchronize with a resource accessible to others.

An Alternative Approach

Although we have disallowed cramming, it should be mentioned that there is a scheduling scheme alternative to the rational method discussed above. This scheme will certainly appeal to the more control-oriented individual, and have an attraction for those who are hopelessly behind as well. (We've also discussed this technique elsewhere, when we decided that in some cases, a job worth doing is worth doing poorly.) In this method, once you've captured your duties and given them their priority score, decide how much time you want to allocate to each. A two-hour task may not be worth two hours, particularly in light of the fact that you have seven more two-hour tasks to complete today. So decide to give it one hour of quality time. You can do this without a great deal of anguish or sense of guilt, because one hour is all you've got to give. With the focus that such an approach demands, you may be surprised by how much you can accomplish during that hour. In software development, this technique is called "time boxing" and is useful because it recognizes and succeeds at meeting hard deadlines.

EVALUATION

How will you know if it's working? Give yourself enough time. It takes at least three weeks to get over the novelty and the discomfort of breaking patterns and beginning to establish a new routine.

Record your reactions in a notebook. You'd be surprised how much your reaction will change in just a few weeks, so much so that you might forget how you felt when you started.

Keep referring to your specific goals. Are you losing that pound and a half a week? Is your new exercise regimen giving you the increased energy and sense of well-being you hoped for?

Evaluate how the change is fitting into the rest of your life. How are your loved ones reacting to the new demand on your time? What have you had to give up to create time for the new activity? Is it a fair tradeoff?

Decide to stick with the plan for another three weeks, make necessary alterations, or scrap the plan and develop a new one. These are your goals, and you have the power to achieve them through specific planning and disciplined action every day. Your priorities and goals may change as your situation changes. As people grow older, for instance, they may have a greater respect for free time and less respect for money. Single people may have different priorities if they marry and have children. The important thing is that we maintain control of our lives by deciding our priorities and how we spend our time. Policies help us to live by design, not by default.

CHAPTER 9

Is It Really Important — or Merely Urgent?

W hat's next?
You face that question hundreds of times each day, from the moment you wake up until you lapse back into sleep. Your answers to those questions determine how you live your life. The sum total of all those answers is your life. As we've seen from the exercise in the previous chapter, you can and need to determine the importance of those questions in order to keep your life in some state of control. Those you can foresee, you can plan and schedule for, but many won't find their way onto your planner.

Many of the questions are pretty basic yes/no decisions.

Shall I get up now or stay in bed for just a few more minutes? Shall I eat breakfast? What shall I eat? Shall I take a shower? What clothes shall I wear?

These aren't really choices, you say? Of course you get up each morning, at pretty much the same time, at least on weekdays. Of course you eat breakfast, or not, as is your custom.

Do you have a choice?

Take the matter of clothes. Your clothes make a statement about your position in society and your attitude toward other people. If I wear a suit, tie, and wingtips, I announce that I'm a solid and productive citizen on my way to business. If I wear a ragged sweatshirt and cutoffs, I still might be a solid citizen, but I'm planning on doing some gardening or washing the car. Black leather, lipstick, and spiked heels make an entirely different statement.

Yes, you say, but you really don't have a lot of choice here, either. Proper business attire is a matter of social convention. True. But you still have a choice. At some point you made that choice consciously. You may now be choosing your level of clothing (if not the specific tie or earrings) by habit or default, but you're still performing an act of free will.

Becoming more conscious of the choices you make and learning to reclaim some of these choices is the very essence of effective time management.

We're not suggesting that you wear leather or cutoffs to business. We're not suggesting that you give a great deal of conscious thought to whether you should brush your teeth, or what toothpaste you should use, or which hand you should hold the toothbrush in, or which quadrant of your mouth you should brush first. You should go right on performing such tasks by rote so long as your routine is effective for you. (And oh the havoc when, for example, you develop carpal tunnel syndrome in your dominant hand and have to try to learn to brush your teeth "wrong-handed.")

But if you're making *all* of your decisions by rote, you're probably not making the best decisions for yourself.

THE DILEMMA OF THE RINGING TELEPHONE

Imagine for a moment that you work in an office and that your office has a telephone (not too much of a stretch there). Imagine that the phone rings (again not a real feat of creative visioning, I suspect). Shall you answer it? Yes, you do have a choice—especially if you have voice mail or can let the call ring through to another phone—but most of us automatically snatch up a ringing phone. (Remember Pavlov and his salivating dogs? And we don't even get a biscuit as a reward when we answer our bells!)

You may have to make the decision to answer a ringing telephone without the most important piece of information, namely, who's on the other end, but let's make it easy by giving you caller ID. Let's suppose that the caller is your significant other (hereafter referred to as the "SO"), the man or woman you share your life with, the single most important person to you on the face of the planet. Now do you want to answer the phone?

Well, sure, of course, except that . . . you *are* at work, and you're awfully busy, right in the middle of something important, on deadline, and, well, truth to tell, you wish you could know what the conversation was to be about before you committed to getting into it, right? Even caller ID can't help you there.

But through the magic of the hypothetical case, I'm going to tell you exactly what your SO wants to talk about and then let you decide whether to pick up that phone or let it ring through. SO is a male in this case, but, obviously, it works either way.

- Case A. SO is calling to tell you that he seems to have lost all feeling on the left side of his face, and he feels as if he might pass out any minute.
- Case B. Your SO just got off the phone after a long talk with his sister, Carol, out in Oregon. She's having a terrible time with her oldest, Bobby, who just got expelled from school for getting caught with marijuana in his locker. Carol's upset, and so's your SO, who doesn't know what he can do to help. He wants to talk to you about it.
- Case C. He wants to talk about your relationship. You had a fight last night, and you were both still upset when you went to work this morning. Some things need ironing out right now.
- Case D. Nothing special. He just wants to chat.

So, are you going to pick up that phone? It's your call (literally). I promise there'll be no repercussions; your SO will never know if you choose to duck him.

No question about Case A, right? You'll not only take the call, but you'll drop whatever you had going at work and race home to take him to the emergency room. Although it's a frightening and potentially horrible situation, it's also an easy decision to make.

Given the circumstances, Case D might be a fairly easy call, too. You'll talk later.

Case B is a little tougher. Of course you care about Carol and Bobby and the whole unfolding soap opera out in Oregon. You care even more that your SO is upset and embroiled in a family problem. But there's certainly nothing you can do about it now (or probably ever, for that matter). And you do have that big meeting in 15 minutes to get ready for.

Do I hear voice mail picking up?

Case C is probably tougher yet. Your relationship with your SO is the most important thing in your life. But this isn't the time, the place, or the medium for a heavy discussion. Rehashing last night's argument now probably won't do any good and might even do some harm. And to tell the truth, you're at least a little angry that he'd call now, knowing how busy you are. And yet . . .

It's probably best to duck this one too so you can discuss the issue when you have the time.

IS IT IMPORTANT OR MERELY URGENT?

It shouldn't be that difficult for you to determine what is important. It was part of the last chapter's exercise, and permitted you to properly prioritize and schedule your tasks. The question of importance is also a personal one and will vary from individual to individual—so it's impossible to define here. If it touches on your core values, the basic motivations that guide your life, it's important. Something is urgent, on the other hand, if it demands your attention right now.

To be an effective time manager, you need to remember the distinction. You also need to remember: Everything that is important is not also necessarily urgent, and everything that is urgent is not necessarily important.

Case A above was an easy decision because the call was both important and urgent to you. The health and safety of a loved one is at stake (or at least seems to be, and there's no way you'd take a chance with something like that), and the situation demands immediate action.

So it is with anything in life that is both important and urgent. Although it may demand a great deal from us, it does not require any decision making.

Case C, the discussion about your relationship, is also clearly quite important but may lack a sense of urgency (why *now*?) or even seem inappropriate (not *now!*).

Case B, with poor Carol and Bobby in Oregon, seems somewhat less important because it's one step removed from your SO, and perhaps even less urgent.

Case D carries with it the least sense of urgency.

There really is an important, maybe even urgent, point to qualifying your decisions. The problem for most of us occurs in categories B and C, the "important but not urgent" and the "urgent but not important." Specifically, you may be spending too much of your time doing the Cs and not enough time on the Bs.

THE SECRET OF TIME MANAGEMENT REVEALED: WHY WE WASTE TIME ON TRIVIA AND DON'T SPEND ENOUGH TIME ON ESSENTIALS

This concept was discussed in depth in Chapter 3, Busy or Productive? So, it's necessary only to point out here that life is full of a series of rapidly occurring urgencies that really don't make any difference in the long run (or even in the short run, for that matter). Yes, you're four minutes late for that department meeting. But the department meeting is a fat waste of everybody's time (including the person running it), ninety minutes of plodding through announcements you could have read for yourself (or chosen to ignore).

Technology has increased our sense of urgency, but the delivery system has no bearing on the importance of the content.

We also have extremely important choices that don't carry with them any sense of urgency. Of course I should exercise regularly. I know it's good for me, mentally as well as physically. And I will. I absolutely will. Just not right now. Hey, I'm four minutes late for the department meeting.

Unless we take conscious control of our decision making, we'll tend to react to the urgent, even if it's relatively unimportant, and shun the important, unless it also carries a sense of urgency.

ASKING THE "WANT TO/HAVE TO" QUESTION

If all this business of dividing activities into four quadrants on an important/urgent grid seems like a lot of work—and it is—here's an easier way to begin to gain control of your daily life.

Again, you're going to need to develop a way to interrupt yourself several times a day. These interruptions can coincide with your mini-vacations, but they don't have to.

Simply stop what you're doing, take a breath, and ask yourself the following:

"Is this what I want or need to be doing right now?"

You can, of course, modify the question to fit your own circumstances and your approach to life. (This version was created by modifying the "Lakein Question" proposed by Alan Lakein in his 1973 book.) But be sure to touch on the three key elements:

Is this what I want
or need
to be doing right now?

Note that it's "or," not "and." Obviously, a task can be a long way from what you'd really like to be doing and still be the thing you need to do.

If the answer to this question is "yes," go back to what you were doing. You will have affirmed your choice of activities and made your decision consciously, the key element in time management.

If you want or need to do it but not right now, put it off and do something with a higher degree of time sensitivity. That way, you'll avoid getting caught in deadline pressure later.

And if you neither want nor need to be doing it, now or ever—STOP!

It may seem amazing to you, but if you consistently practice the "want/need" question, you really will catch yourself doing things you can't justify doing on any grounds, and you'll find yourself shifting activities to better serve your needs.

This simple question can make a tremendous positive difference in the way you live.

KNOWING WHEN TIME ISN'T REALLY THE PROBLEM

To get the whole picture, we need to reiterate one more element here:

Time management isn't always a matter of time at all.

Going to that department meeting and sitting in a passive stupor is neither important nor particularly pleasurable (unless you're a gifted daydreamer), but it is a lot *easier* than exercising.

Confronting the office deadline may be a lot easier for many of us than trying to iron out the kinks in our relationships. Often we will take the path of least resistance, especially if we can justify the choice on grounds other than ease. (I *have* to go to the meeting. It's my job.)

WHY YOU'LL NEVER BE ABLE TO "FIND" TIME

Time only needs "managing" because we don't seem to have enough time to do everything we want and need to do. In particular, we never seem able to "find time" for those important but not urgent activities.

Stop looking. You'll never *find* time. It isn't lost. You're living it. You have to consciously decide to live it in certain ways and not others. You have to *make* time by taking it away from one activity and giving it to another.

Conscientious and creative use of the to-do list can help here. If you want to exercise three times a week, if you need to do some long-range career and financial planning, if you care enough about another human being to want to nurture your relationship, you will schedule time for these things. Otherwise, you may not "get to them," and even if you do, you'll give them only your leftover time, when energy and focus are at their lowest.

You can make time for the important things in life by reducing time spent on the items in the last category, the "neither important nor urgent" area. But you shouldn't wipe this area out completely because there are a number of activities, things we do for fun or just for the heck of it, that fall here.

CHAPTER 10

Ways to Avoid Time Traps

Few of us work in a vacuum. Most of us have contact with our colleagues every day, either one-on-one or in group meetings. We spend a considerable amount of time conversing, sharing information, negotiating for resources, presenting ideas, providing status reports, getting feedback, solving problems, establishing or reinforcing team units—as well as just shooting the bull—on an informal and formal basis.

Yet when the amount of time spent in meetings is weighed against the results from these meetings, it's clear that a good portion of that time is unproductive. Statistics show that the time we spent meeting is increasing while the satisfaction we feel is decreasing. It's a problem that has spawned seminars and consultants aplenty with a host of observations, rules, and the serious prospect for more meetings.

THE ONE-ON-ONE MEETING

The single greatest potential time exploiter for most of us comes in the form of the colleague who, discovering he needs some last-minute information to finish his current task, telephones or stops by and asks the simple question: "Got a minute?" We can normally sympathize with this colleague because we frequently are guilty of this behavior as well. But, while we should be aware that burning one's bridges can be costly, we still need to consider our answer to this question before responding automatically in the affirmative. Once we say "Now's fine" or "What can I do for you?" we've signed a blank check and the caller gets to fill in the amount.

Those three innocent little words—"Got a minute?"—may be stealing your life, a few minutes at a time.

You can stop this time-erosion, and you can probably do it without hurting anybody's feelings. But hurt feelings or not, you need to take back control of your day.

Let's take it from the top, from the moment somebody asks "Got a minute?" and see if we can work out a response someplace between, "Why, sure. Take all you want" and "Buzz off."

WHAT'S WRONG WITH "BUZZ OFF"?

It won't win you many friends—or customers, of course. But beyond that, it may be inappropriate. You may want and need to have the conversation being offered you.

You have the right to decide.

That's the key to effective time management in a sentence. You have the right to decide how you spend your time, which is to say that you have the right to decide what you'll do this minute.

To make an intelligent decision, you need two critical pieces of information:

1. What does the caller want to talk about?
2. How much time does the caller want to talk about it?

When you have this information, you can decide if and, if so, how long to talk.

You have the right to ask.

In fact, you're not very smart if you don't.

There are lots of nice ways to do it. "How may I help you?" is a good one, since it focuses on the needs of the caller while eliciting the information you need. You can no doubt come up with several more to fit various situations. If you need to, write them down on a 6 × 9 card and keep them by the phone as a reminder and a cue card until you feel natural asking.

WHAT ABOUT THAT OLD STANDBY, "NO"?

Is it ever okay simply to answer "Got a minute?" with "No"?

Of course. You get to decide, remember? If you really don't have a minute, "No" is the proper as well as the accurate response.

You can follow it up, as well as soften an abrupt and seemingly insensitive response, by buying a little time ("Can I get back to you in about half an hour?") or by setting a specific time to talk. That way, you've asserted control over your schedule, which is to say, your life.

Note, though, that you've still signed a blank check; you've just postdated it. You still don't know what the conversation is about or how long it will take, and you still don't know if you really want or need to have the conversation at all.

THE GOLDEN RULE APPLIED TO THREE LITTLE WORDS

If you practice effective responses to "Got a minute?" long enough, you'll train some of your frequent interrupters to ask the right question in the first place, a question that will supply the information you need to answer it.

"I need about five minutes to discuss the Anderson project with you. Is this a good time?" How about you? Is that the way you open a conversation, or are you just as guilty of the "Got a minute?" gaff as everyone else? Get in the practice of asking-as-you-would-be-asked. You'll get a lot better response.

But don't bother trying to teach the rest of the world to practice proper etiquette in the workplace. You're in charge of your life, not theirs. Besides, you probably won't convert anybody, and the effort won't make you very popular.

Consider this: it may be somebody else's *fault* for asking the wrong question, but it's your *responsibility* to take care of your own time.

THE GROUP MEETING

Those who make predictions about such things predicted that video conferencing would become extremely popular, replacing many face-to-face meetings. It's an attractive concept for lots of reasons, not the least of which is the time savings potential for meeting participants who are spared the need to travel. But video conferencing hasn't yet reached the potential its advocates had hoped for, and may not until it can overcome some of its awkward and unnatural qualities. We prefer, at least for the time being, the ability to make eye contact with our colleagues, to see and judge their expressions and gestures up close in a face-to-face, live context.

So, reports of the death of meetings are premature. Meetings will continue to be a prominent part of the landscape for most knowledge workers, and at certain levels of responsibility, can consume more than half the work week.

Just as with the one-on-one, impromptu meeting, the more formal, scheduled, multi-participant meeting should be approached with the cold, objective point-of-view that considers: What can I gain from attending this meeting? and What will I miss (or what other tasks can I spend the time doing?) if I don't attend? Before you can answer those questions, you need to know:

1. What's the subject matter?
2. How long will the meeting last?
3. Am I the right person? (Actually, Phyllis is handling that account. You'd better ask her.)
4. Does it really require a meeting? (Maybe a two-minute discussion among the principals, or a couple of e-mails will resolve the issue so we can avoid having to meet later.)

Knowing the answers to these questions will permit you to decide whether to accept the invitation or decline. If the report you've been working on for two weeks must be circulated at close of business today, you really don't have the luxury of spending three hours discussing a new project that may not be your responsibility anyway. You find with profound regret that your schedule does not permit you to attend, but you hope for a most productive meeting and want to be kept informed of the results.

The reality of the situation may be somewhat different. You won't always have the ability to duck a meeting. Attendance is expected at your department meetings, for example, and when your manager puts you on the list for a meeting, you'd better have a bona fide reason that he will accept if you plan to skip. You also should consider, when you're thinking about what a pointless waste of time the planning committee meeting is, what you'll miss if you don't attend. It's easy to find yourself outside the loop, and even if most attendees seem critical of each other, meetings can also cement or repair bonds between colleagues. Miss too many and you run the risk of finding yourself marginalized.

MAXIMIZE YOUR MEETING PRODUCTIVITY

Since meetings are a part of the work environment, and you know how to diplomatically avoid those that result in a net loss of information and/or kill brain cells, you are left with the responsibility to attend an abundance of meetings. Some tips, truths, and guidelines for survival in meeting mode:

1. Don't set up a meeting merely to distribute information; use email. Summarize the important points so no one will miss them, and circulate the complete report for people who need all the facts.
2. No meeting should be planned or attended that doesn't have an agenda and schedule including ending time. (See also the discussion of reality above.)
3. The best meeting agendas include the expected outcome or decisions. This alerts attendees that they're not meeting to just discuss, but are expected to deliver a result.

4. Even if it isn't your meeting, you should be fully prepared to discuss the topic(s) and have information to back up your points. You weren't invited just to look pretty.

5. Most meetings, unless they require maximum creative input, should be scheduled in the afternoon. Most people are more mentally alert and productive in the morning, and should use that time on important tasks.

6. Start the meeting on time. Inform late-comers what topic is under discussion, but don't back up and don't apologize. Respect the time of those who are punctual.

7. Results of every meeting should be recorded—decisions reached, actions required, individuals responsible for the actions, and their expected completion dates. Attendees and stakeholders should receive a summary of the results after the meeting.

8. If the group has made a decision to assign an action to an individual, but there is disagreement about what that action involves, don't spend meeting time discussing it. Ask interested parties to send suggestions directly to the person responsible. Most will lose their passion when the audience disperses.

9. Don't use the meeting to discuss new business. End promptly and schedule another meeting if necessary.

10. The agenda for a problem-solving meeting should request each participant to bring a possible solution to the meeting. The better informed and prepared each attendee is, the more productive the meeting will be.

11. Encourage all attendees to contribute their opinions, even if contentious, as long as they are to the point. Don't ridicule any ideas, don't criticize any participants. Most people want to conform with others, but creative ideas come from a environment that fosters diversity and individual expression without fear of reprisal.

12. Don't let participants ramble or get off the subject. The meeting leader has a responsibility to keep the meeting under control and on subject.

13. If the meeting's goal is to resolve a dispute, sit near or have eye contact with your allies, and try to separate your opponents.

14. Review the meeting's results at its conclusion so that future meetings can be improved.

15. Try to keep the number of meeting attendees to a maximum of eight.

16. Don't waste time on visual aids if they're not visual and dramatic, if they are hard to read or understand, or if the information is more effectively rendered in written handouts.

17. Don't hesitate to schedule a meeting when necessary. If problems crop up and hard decisions are needed, it's better to get the principals together and solve the problem quickly.

CHAPTER 11

Seven Time Management Tips for Managers

M anaging people takes time. It may take inefficient or inef-
fective managers longer to plan, supervise, and evaluate
someone else's work than to just do the work themselves.
The answer isn't to fire the staff. The answer is to manage them more
effectively. Here are seven time management tips that will help you do it.

1. NEVER WASTE THEIR TIME

Does the sight of one of your workers standing idle threaten you? If
so, resist the temptation to assign busy work just to keep your staff
moving. You waste their time and your own. If it's a task that's not
important for you to be doing, it's not important for your staff either.

You'll also be eroding their trust in you and your decisions.
They know it's busy work!

Don't fill their time for them. Show them what needs doing.
Show them how to do it. Make sure they have the tools they need.
Then get out of the way, but don't disappear. You are interested in
the results of their work; ask for feedback, but not as a means to
micromanage. Don't interrupt them needlessly.

If one or more employees are continually idle, it may not be their
fault; they are either more efficient than you thought, or they just don't
have enough work to keep them busy. It's time to reevaluate their duties,
but don't punish them for working hard or your own poor planning.

2. MAKE SURE THE TIME SAVERS ARE REALLY SAVING THEIR TIME

Many of us have witnessed the introduction of a new business
process, an improved method for accomplishing some task. These

improvements often are part of a package purchased by management from consultants who were retained to find solutions to waste or inefficiencies. Typically, a simple task involving a form that captures a schedule or some repetitive action becomes a Web-based process. Now the information can be managed, combined, compared, analyzed, archived, and made accessible to anyone who wants it. The price paid for the power this new process offers is normally the extra time spent entering and editing the data, applying the correct codes, and filling in all the required fields. Somewhere in the organization, someone benefits by having this information in a new, accessible format, and for the rest of us, well . . . we are usually not given a choice.

As a manager whose task it is to promulgate company policies, objecting to or resisting these changes is not only a waste of effort, but also a sure way to destroy your image as a team player. If you have input in the decision-making process that results in the adoption of new methods, it behooves you to raise the issue of time as a factor; too often it is overlooked in the organization's zeal to reap promised rewards. If your staff needs to learn and implement a system more cumbersome than that used previously, your managers need to understand and appreciate its effects on your team's productivity. It also helps your staff if they understand the reasons for the change, particularly if the benefits are not obvious to them.

3. SEPARATE THE IMPORTANT FROM THE MERELY URGENT FOR YOUR STAFF

For your staff, as for yourself, you need to distinguish between truly important activities, those that serve the central mission, and the stuff that seems to demand immediate attention without really meriting it.

Ask "Why?" for the phone calls and memos and e-mails demanding your staff's immediate attention. Can you relieve some of the pressure and release your staffers for more important work? And let them know you are on their side in reducing the busy work.

Delegate interesting assignments, ones that stretch imagination and creativity, and encourage personal and professional growth.

Do you and your staff ever engage in long-term planning, skills training, or needed conflict management? Or do these things get lost in the daily clamor?

You'll never "find" time to do these vital (but seldom urgent) activities with your staff. As a good manager, you must be sure to make the time. As you schedule these activities, you'll find that staff becomes better at managing their own time, more mission-oriented and future-thinking. You're training them to improve quality, not just quantity.

4. TELL THEM WHY

"Why do I have to do this?"

If that question from a staffer feels like a threat to your authority, if you become defensive when you hear such a question, your staffers will learn to keep the questions to themselves.

But they'll still wonder.

They have the right and the need to know the purpose of their work. When you ask them to do something, give them a good reason.

You'll have a more motivated and more efficient workforce if they understand the goals and not just the process.

5. ALLOW THEM ENOUGH TIME FOR THE TASK

Be realistic in your demands. Never put "ASAP" on assignments—instead indicate a specific date that assignments are to be completed. Don't overstuff the staff. If you do, you'll get shoddy work. You might even get less work. Even a conscientious, willing worker does not perform well under unreasonable pressure. And you will gain the reputation of being unreasonable. On longer assignments, consult with your staff to determine a reasonable due date.

6. ENCOURAGE THEM TO DO ONE THING WELL—AT A TIME

Watch your staff at work. Are they on the phone, jotting notes, eyeing the computer screen, all while trying to grab a fast sandwich?

Getting a lot done? Probably not. And they're probably not getting anything done well.

If your coworker is on the phone with a potential client, you want that worker's total attention on the task at hand, not thinking about the next project or the last project or the work that isn't getting done.

They'll work faster and better, with less need for clarification during or revision later.

7. HAVE PRODUCTIVE STAFF MEETINGS

Ask your staff to make a list of things they least like to do and chances are "go to a meeting" will rank right up there with "take work home over the weekend."

Most of us hate meetings, and with good reason. We avoid them if we can, resent them when we can't, and complain about them before, during, and after. That's because most meetings are a waste of time, too often involving certain individuals talking to hear themselves talk.

But, you really do need staff meetings. You can create a productive interaction that just doesn't occur with memos or e-mails or phone calls or one-on-one conversations. People get a better grasp of the whole operation. Names become faces, and faces become individuals. You can develop and maintain a sense of shared purpose and cooperation. In a meeting:

- Everyone hears the same thing at the same time, removing some (but, alas, not all) miscommunication.
- If people don't understand, they can ask for clarification.
- The speaker can use nonverbal clues (crossed arms, frowns, glazed eyes, eager nodding) to determine how people are responding to a proposal.

- Most important, when people interact, they create ideas that never would have occurred otherwise.

Schedule regular meetings. If you don't have a reason to meet, or if you have reasons not to meet, you can always cancel. Nobody ever complains about a canceled meeting, do they?

But every time you do have a meeting, make it worth their time and energy to be there.

Here's how.

1. Get ready.

You really have to know your stuff to explain it to others. Do your homework. Review your reason(s) for holding the meeting and the outcome(s) you want.

2. Get the meeting place ready.

Make sure you've got the flipchart and markers and overhead projector. How about visuals? Refreshments? Put them around a table.

3. Get them ready.

Don't pass out copies of a thick report to start the meeting and then expect folks to read and react on the spot. Even the most willing worker won't be able to do a good job.

What do they need to know before the meeting? Get information to them at least two working days ahead of time. Sure, some won't read it. But many will, and they'll come prepared.

4. Get out an agenda.

Whatever else you send them before the meeting, be sure to circulate an agenda. Emphasize action items and spell out the results expected from the meeting. If they need to bring something with them (like their calendars, so you can plan yet another meeting), tell them now. Make sure all participants have a role.

Be sure to indicate a reminder of the day, place, and time on the agenda.

5. Get rid of bad talk; promote good talk.

Don't let your meeting degenerate into personal attack or serve as a forum for griping. Do not assign blame or allow others to. Encourage the sharing of ideas and suggestions that promote the mission or improve the process. Give praise and support pride and positive team attitudes. Share and celebrate achievements.

Here are a few ground rules other groups have found helpful:

- Use "I" statements in sharing your perceptions. Don't say: "This meeting is a stupid waste of time"; instead say: "I feel like we're wasting our time here."
- Talk about issues, not personalities. Don't say: "Your idea is idiotic"; instead say: "I don't think this idea will work because . . ."
- Come prepared.
- Listen actively. Don't interrupt.
- Don't yell, pound the table, or curse.

You might not want or need these guidelines. Develop your own to work for your group.

Now what do we do?

So what are you going to do with all this time you've saved for your staff? You probably won't have trouble filling the time. But if you don't plan for it, existing jobs will simply expand to fill it.

Your final task as an effective time manager for your staff must be to consider how time really ought to be spent. Are there other important activities that haven't been getting done?

Before you spend all their time, though, consider giving a little time off as a reward for a job well done, ahead of schedule. You can't give them anything they'll appreciate more and that could motivate them better.

CHAPTER 12

Learning to Say "No"

Are you one of those busy people who can always be counted on to take on an additional job? You'll not only serve on the volunteer board, you'll chair it, take the meeting notes, edit the newsletter, and head up the recruitment subcommittee.

"I just don't know how you do it all," folks tell you.

Do you? Do you know *why* you do? And have you considered how much that extra work is costing you?

"I just don't have your energy," folks tell you, or "I can't ever seem to find the time"—right before they ask you to take on another job.

"We can always count on you!" they gush when you say "yes."

Your willingness to serve speaks well for you. You help because you believe in the cause and because you want to make your family, your workplace, and your community better places. You're a helper, a problem solver, a doer. You're community-minded, a team player, in sports parlance the "go-to person."

But you may be doing more than you should—for your own physical and mental health, for the well-being of your loved ones, and for your ability to be effective and efficient. To find out, examine your motives—all of them—for saying "yes" to each task.

WHY WE MAY HAVE TROUBLE SAYING "NO"

1. Looking for love in all the right causes. You do indeed earn the gratitude and approval of your peers when you shoulder their burdens. The need for their approval and acceptance may in part be the reason you say "yes."

Behind this desire may even lurk the fear that, if you don't work so hard, those around you will stop accepting you.

2. The guilt syndrome. "It's difficult to say 'no' when someone asks you to serve on a not-for-profit board, or chair a committee, or attend a fund-raiser for a very worthy cause," writes Jan Benson Wright, editor of *The Peoria Woman*. "When we decline, we are often inclined to shoulder a subsequent burden of guilt, because 'superwoman' failed to come through as expected." Sometimes that guilt can cloud our objectivity.

3. The myth of indispensability. Rather than kindness, your effort may in part be motivated by arrogance. Perhaps you don't let others do the job because, deep down, you don't believe anyone else can do it or do it as well as you can. You've taken to heart the adage "If you want a job done right, do it yourself."

4. The fear of expendability. What if you didn't show up for work and nobody noticed? On some basic, subconscious level, you may be afraid that the moment you stop all your efforts, people will discover that they don't really need you at all. Or, you may feel this on a very conscious and practical level, and need to reinforce your importance to your organization.

5. The Martyr Syndrome. Do you secretly enjoy bearing the burdens of an overworked schedule? Do you believe that it's your lot in life to suffer—in a time management sense?

Reasons three and four may seem mutually exclusive, but they're not. It's quite possible to feel both ways at the same time. Just as you can be in a "love/hate relationship," you can feel both indispensable and expendable.

If any of these motivations apply to you, and you're able to admit it, you may be saying "yes" because it satisfies some need or quells a fear more painful than the loss of time from accepting more duties.

Understanding this about yourself is the first big step in summoning the courage to say "no."

WHY ALL THAT "YES" SNEAKS UP ON YOU

Glaucoma is a gradual hardening of the eyeball, which if left untreated, can cause blindness. It's an especially insidious disease; because the impairment is so gradual, the victim is often able to make subtle, unconscious compensations for a slowly shrinking field of vision, becoming aware of the disease only when it's too late to treat it.

Making too many commitments can be like that, too.

"The problem with clutter in our lives, like clutter in our closets, is it arrives one piece at a time, never in basketfuls," Benson Wright notes. "It's not too difficult to refuse a huge, overwhelming load of additional responsibilities; it's tough, however, to decline 'just one more.'"

Add up all the extra tasks you perform, anything above and beyond what's required. Check your planner and look closely at time slots in the evening and on weekends, your "personal" time.

Here's the start of one person's list:

- Coach a Y basketball team
- Chair the workplace expectations committee at the office
- Coordinate United Way fundraising in the department
- Serve as recording secretary for the church council
- And on and on . . .

These are all good, worthwhile things to do. Somebody should do them. But does it have to be *you* in every instance?

The items on your list are all good, worthy endeavors, too. You probably genuinely enjoy doing them. We tend to enjoy the things we do well and gravitate toward these tasks when we have a choice. Time management would be a lot easier if there were obvious time wasters on your list and tasks you dreaded doing.

HOW MANY JOBS DO YOU HAVE?

Your list of extra commitments may not be complete. You also need to figure in jobs you've taken on that rightfully belong to someone else—not some generic "other person" who could take over as committee chair if you stepped down, but the specific person whose job you've shouldered.

Connie hates to write up the required sales reports at the end of each day. She'd much rather be out in the field making more sales. You really don't mind the paperwork, and actually, you seem to have a flair for it. Yes, it's an extra hour or so at the office, but you really don't mind.

Everyone is supposed to take a turn making the coffee at the office, but . . . Jeff makes it too strong. Sylvia never washes out the pot when it's empty. Nora leaves the machine on overnight. Gloria forgets when it's her turn. It's easier if you just go ahead and make the damned coffee!

A QUALITATIVE METHOD FOR COMPUTING THE COST OF YOUR COMMITMENTS

Got your list finished? (Don't worry. You can always add items as you think of them.) Now it's time to figure out what all that activity really costs you.

You probably have a good idea how much money you give to charitable causes. Many of us come up with a fairly precise number to report to the IRS every April 15th. This calculation enables you to make adjustments in next year's giving, bringing the level up or down to where you think it ought to be and redistributing funds according to your shifting awareness and priorities.

But most of us aren't nearly as conscious of how much time we're donating. This lack of awareness makes it much harder to change your level of involvement or redistribute your energies.

Put some numbers next to the items on your activity list. Estimate the amount of time you spend in a week, a month, or perhaps a year. You don't need mathematical precision here, but you do need honesty. Don't fudge.

When you add up those numbers, you begin to get a sense of how much your perpetual motion is costing you.

Money has value in terms of what it will buy for us (possessions, comfort, status, entertainment, relative freedom . . .). Same with time; we only truly appreciate its value in terms of what we can do with it.

What would you be doing if you weren't doing some of the activities on your list? We carry around a lot of "if only's . . . ," things we say we'd do if only we could find the time. Make a list of your "if only's . . ." Here are some examples:

If only I could find the time, I'd . . .
learn how to play golf
learn new skills to help me advance at work
get more sleep
master conversational Spanish
earn an M.B.A.
have people over for dinner at least twice a month

Perhaps you don't really want to *learn* Spanish; you simply wish you knew how to *speak* Spanish. The first is active; you'd really enjoy the process of learning. The second is passive; you wish you already had the benefit of the activity. Even so, you may be willing to do the work to get the benefit. If so, leave the item on your list.

Take a good look at your list. It represents the true cost of your commitments. Line up the two lists, commitments on the left, yearnings on the right. Decide which activity on the commitment list you'll quit and which activity on the wish list you'll begin instead. Then do whatever it takes to make the switch.

ANOTHER SUBJECTIVE METHOD FOR TRIMMING THE ACTIVITY LIST

Go through your activity list twice more. On the first pass through, assign a number from 1 to 10 for each on the enjoyment scale, 10 being "highly pleasurable," and 1 being "pure drudgery." Then go through again, assigning a number from 1 to 10 on the importance scale, 10 being "crucial to the survival of the human race" (well, maybe not quite that important), 1 being "nobody really cares."

Our hypothetical list of activities might look like this:

ACTIVITY	ENJOYMENT	IMPORTANCE
Coach a Y basketball team	9	7
Chair the workplace expectations committee at the office	2	4
Coordinate United Way fundraising in the department	1	8
Serve as recording secretary for the church council	5	5

Just looking at the numbers, it seems we've got ourselves a basketball coach here. If you give it a 9 on the enjoyment scale, you're probably also good at doing it. (That correlation doesn't always work, but it's an awfully strong indicator.) If you like it, you're good at it, *and* you think it's important, do it!

Want something to trim? I think it's time the workplace expectations committee found itself a new chair, don't you?

The United Way job is tougher to call. It may be extremely important, but you may not be the person to do it. The cold truth is, someone else who enjoys coordinating and fundraising will probably do a much better job than you will.

THE "SOMETHING'S GOT TO GIVE" THEORY OF TIME MANAGEMENT

The next time someone asks you to take on a new activity . . .
The next time you find yourself starting to take over a task
without even being asked . . .
The next time you're tempted for any reason to take on a new
commitment . . .

Write the task on your commitment list and, next to it, write the specific activity you're going to give up to do it. Again, you need to be honest here; the time it took you to perform the old activity must equal the time required for the new one.

Here are some examples:

NEW ACTIVITY	OLD ACTIVITY
Exercise on the treadmill (45 minutes every morning)	45 minutes of sleep
Chair the neighborhood recycling committee	Play with my kids on those Saturday mornings
Join a book discussion group (two-hour meeting each month, ten hours to read the book)	Watch television (three hours/ week)

The first tradeoff, exercise for sleep, may not be a good deal (although it's one that many of us happily have made). Exercise is surely good for physical, mental, and emotional well-being. But so is sleep. Are you getting enough? Too much? Not enough (more likely)?

If you decide you need the sleep, that doesn't mean you can't also do the exercise. It means you have to figure out another trade.

The second tradeoff is even more problematic. You may believe strongly that recycling is our last best chance to save the planet. But you also place high value on spending time with your kids, especially if you don't get to see them much during the week. Can you work another trade? You'd have to find a way that would also fit the kids' "schedules," of course. (Don't decide to give up watching *Saturday Night Live* to play with your four-year-old.)

Can't find a way to do the recycling without abandoning the kids? Then you might have to leave the recycling to somebody else.

The third example looks like a terrific swap. Instead of wasting time on mindless television, you'll be exercising your critical skills and absorbing great literature. Maybe. But television and print are simply media of expression. The content surely has to factor into the equation. Are you giving up reruns of a sitcom to read genuinely stimulating books? Go for it. But swapping concert performances on television for works of breathy romance may not be a great deal. (I'm not saying it isn't. It's a matter of taste.)

To do this right, you should figure in the quality of that two-hour group discussion, too. Are you having a good time in the company of stimulating conversationalists, or do you come home fuming over all those "nitwitted numbskulls" in your reading group?

HEARTLESS OR PRACTICAL?

All this computing of relative worth may seem cold and calculating, and you do risk squeezing all the spontaneity out of life if you always draw up a list before you act. (I have a friend who put together a "pro" and "con" list of reasons to leave his wife. Now that's heartless. But I digress.) This objective figuring is in fact a way to heed your heart by giving more time to activities that support your core values.

You would never consciously choose to neglect your kids. But you might choose to spend less time with them by default, without realizing you were doing so, when you take on the socially worthy work of being your neighborhood recycling czar. Well-meaning resolutions to "make it up to them" might quiet your conscience, but it probably won't translate into actual time spent.

HOW TO SAY "NO"

All this figuring and calculating and deciding won't do you a bit of good if you aren't able to act on your decisions.

The moment is at hand. The out-going chair (desperate to find a replacement) has asked you to shoulder the burden. What do you say?

1. Beware the automatic "yes." You may have gotten into your time-crunch because you have a very hard time saying "no." But you've learned by bitter experience that it's much harder to get out of something later than to turn it down now. And, you're trying to face up to your inner demons.
2. Buy time. Unless you're already certain of your response one way or the other, ask for time to think about it. This is both a reasonable and a truthful response. You really do want and need time to think about it (if not to pull out various lists and rating scales). Realize, however, that you will have to respond eventually, and by delaying your response, you may have created a situation in which others believe that you have tacitly agreed. Your delay also may make it very difficult ultimately to decline because no time is left to recruit a replacement.
3. If the answer is "no," say "no." Say it gracefully, but say it.

"I'm really flattered that you'd think of me. Thank you so much. But I'm going to have to turn the opportunity down."
And then shut up!

4. Deflect the conversation. Decline the offer and suggest an alternative.

"Thank you for thinking of me, but I'm going to have to decline. I bet Bill would be perfect for the job, don't you?"

This technique works best, obviously, if Bill is not part of the conversation and cannot object. It immediately turns the attention from you to another victim. Even if poor Bill is elsewhere at the moment, however, he will undoubtedly learn and may even resent you for so graciously volunteering his services. So, this may save you time but cost you an ally in the long run.

5. You don't have to give a reason. This may come as a shock. We're reasonable people. We like to think we're motivated by reason, and we want others to understand and agree with our rationale for our decisions. We want people to continue to think well of us. So we share our reasons. And when we do, we invite others to participate in a discussion.

"I'm just too busy right now."

"I know how busy you are. But actually this doesn't take very much time at all. And besides, you're so efficient and well-organized. . . ."

"I really don't think I'm the best choice for the job."

"You're just being modest. You're perfect for the job. Why, with your way with people and your ability to handle a meeting. . . ."

You'll lose this debate. You're arguing the negative position, often a much harder stance to support logically. You can be rationally talked out of something you feel strongly to be right and talked into something you know instinctively to be wrong for you.

If you "lose" (meaning you fail to get them to say, "You're right. Sorry I asked"), you've got two alternatives, neither of them good. You can acquiesce and agree to take on the task. Or you can stick to your guns and continue to say "No," leaving both of you much more upset than necessary.

Decide, based on your informed understanding of your motives and the true costs and benefits of the activity. Then stick to your decision! You'll find yourself with a great deal more conscious control of your life.

CHAPTER 13

Communications

All of us communicate, and many of us communicate in writing. We may not write books—or even annual reports or business plans. But we write memos, letters, work orders, presentations, directions, equipment orders, job evaluations, responses to job evaluations, resumes, contracts, and a lot of other attempts at assembling words in a logical order so they'll make sense—the sense we intend—for the reader.

But unlike professional writers who make their living by writing, most of us do a lot of other things every day. We can't afford to spend a lot of time with writing. We also can't afford the time it takes to do it over and to clear up the confusion and misunderstandings created by poor written communication. Even if we had the time, we may not be aware that our communications are not communicating. Yet in a study conducted by Microsoft in 2005, 39 percent of workers cite lack of team communication as a time waster responsible for decreased productivity.

To help those of us without formal training in the art, following is some advice that may prove helpful.

TIPS FOR WRITING IT RIGHT—AND FAST—THE FIRST TIME

1. Start at the End

What is the purpose of your document and who is your audience? You should know precisely what you hope to accomplish before you start writing or you might as well not bother. Answering these questions will enable you to determine what information to include and what you can leave out, what points to emphasize, and in what order they need to be presented. The reader should also be clear about the document's purpose from the start.

2. Keep It Short and Simple

The Ten Commandments required fewer than 300 words, and Abe Lincoln only needed 271 for the Gettysburg Address. You should try to express yourself in as few words as possible, saving your time and the reader's. Remember that attention spans are short, and getting shorter.

Cut out each and every word that you don't really, really, really need. Don't even say "in order to" if a simple "to" will do.

Make your words easy to read by highlighting the main ideas. You can emphasize an idea by

- putting it first;
- using underlining, boldface, or larger type;
- breaking a list out from paragraph form with bullets (you're reading one now);
- breaking thoughts into separate sections with subtitles.

Eschew obfuscation. Pardon me. I mean keep it simple and clear.

Plain talk is always best. Simple, direct language takes less time to compose and less time to understand.

When you encounter a document bristling with ponderous terminology, you can be fairly certain that it was written by a committee, is a government product, or the author has something to hide. Unless you fall into one of those categories, keep it simple.

3. Get Off to a Flying Start

Formal outlines are a waste of time unless the outline is going to become part of the document, or if that's how you happen to think best. Otherwise, if you need to organize your thoughts before you write, create a mind map. Identify your subject and write it in the center of a sheet of paper. Put down the major points you want to make, and connect them to the subject by lines. Attach reminders about data, anecdotes, and examples you'll want to use to the appropriate major points with other lines. Number the points in the order you want them to appear.

If you prefer, you can use information management software for this purpose. Some of it works in exactly the same way as the paper method, by letting us visualize what we wish to communicate. Use the method that's most convenient and natural—the electronic format is handy because it captures thoughts so they can be used for the next step. It is also helpful, in the hands of an accomplished user, to capture the ideas of a group of people during a brainstorming session, and to share those ideas with others.

Using an outline or a mind map, you now have captured and roughly organized all the ideas you need to include. If you need more information, you'll discover that now (rather than halfway through the project). When you're ready to go, you'll know exactly where you're going.

Now engage in a little flash keyboarding. Just let the words fly, without worrying about punctuation, spelling, or sentence structure. The important point is to capture the essence of each idea and the flow between ideas.

You'll need to go back and edit, of course, but the time it takes to key a rough (very rough) draft and then edit it will be less—possibly much less—than you would have taken pushing your way along, word by tortured word, trying to create perfection as you go.

4. Sustain the Flow

Take breaks before you need them. Writing is one of the most tiring things you can do while sitting down. Don't wait until you're exhausted. Stretch, take a walk, get some water, and return to the battle.

Don't wait until you're stuck to stop, either for a break or at the end of a day's session. If you do, you'll carry a sense of dread around with you. When you sit down to begin again, you'll have a tough time getting started.

Break knowing exactly how you'll continue. Jot yourself a few notes on the next two or three points you want to make. You'll be ready to start without a warm-up.

5. Finish Cleanly

You've said what you needed to say. Now you need to come up with the Big Finish, right?

Wrong.

Trying to come up with an important-sounding conclusion is another waste of time. You are not trying to impress anyone with your literary prowess. This is business. If the piece of writing is long, reiterate the main idea or recap the main points. If it's short, simply end strongly with your final point. Make sure that the reader takes away the conclusion you intended.

6. Edit by the Numbers

You've written quickly—and the writing shows it. You've got some editing to do.

If possible, arrange your work schedule so that you can set the just-completed document aside and do something else before you try to revise. That usually means getting the rough draft done far enough ahead of deadline, and that's a matter of good planning.

The cooling-off period will allow you to gain some objectivity (although you will never be totally objective about your own work, and you shouldn't be).

Pull out your mind map to make sure you've captured all the points you planned to, and nothing extraneous has crept in. If you find that you've recorded random thoughts unrelated to the subject, cut them out regardless of how beautifully they're expressed. Put yourself in the reader's position and think about the questions she might ask; make sure they're answered.

Now go over whatever remains, using a checklist of the specific problems you need to look for, misspellings and dangling modifiers, maybe, and also the almost-right word, the soft passive voice construction, the vague reference.

Where will you get such a checklist? You'll create one by keeping a pad of paper with you as you edit the next couple of pieces you've written, noting the sorts of mistakes you tend to make. That's another one of those forward-thinking tasks that takes extra time now but will save a great deal of time later.

If you want a reference to help you with the editing, keep the *Associated Press Style Book* handy to settle questions such as 6:00 a.m., 6:00 A.M., 6:00 A.M., or 6:00 am, for example. For grammar and structure questions, you can rely on *The Elements of Style,* by Will Strunk and E. B. White. Whatever style guide you use, remember that consistency is usually more important. Readers can adjust to the way in which something is expressed (with the possible exception of typos), but it tries the patience if the reader is asked to continually readjust.

A CAUTIONARY NOTE ABOUT EDITING

Don't even think about not doing it.

You'll save a little time, all right. But you'll spend that time and more, writing the second and third memo clarifying the first one, holding the meeting to explain what you really meant, or explaining to the boss why your report caused the client to cancel the contract. No amount of time or effort will salvage your damaged reputation.

Even simple typos make your judgments questionable and your reasoning suspect. For important documents, employ a colleague or friend to edit, and then listen and take seriously any criticism. It's too easy to pass off the opinion of someone by telling yourself that he just doesn't understand what you're trying to say. Exactly. Others won't either. Build time into the schedule for this edit and the rewrite.

A FEW CAUTIONS ABOUT INSTANT WRITING

We've come a long way from the days of communicating with letters chiseled on stone tablets or scrawled with sticks in the dirt. Today's preferred method, e-mail, offers so many advantages and is so firmly entrenched in business culture that it's impossible to conduct business without it. But in view of the suggestions for good business writing we just discussed, it's worth noting several characteristics about e-mail that counter these writing techniques.

E-mail liabilities include:

- Because you can send it so fast, you can send it too fast (and wish you hadn't).

The need for speed, enabled by the e-mail medium, encourages us to write without considering a message's effect—on the recipient, on others who receive a copy, or on others unknown to you who may be copied now or at a later time. It's worthwhile to take a moment to think about a message's tone—ask a colleague if the topic warrants it—before firing off that reply.

- A "private" e-mail message is not private.

Paper has a way of falling into the wrong hands sometimes, too. The problem here is that e-mail creates the illusion of privacy. But the e-mail system is a business resource, and all the messages sent are the property of the business. Think about all those e-mails that turn up at trials. E-mails also can easily be sent to the wrong people. The stories of e-mails inadvertently sent to unintended recipients—hitting "reply all" instead of "reply" is the classic method—are legendary and quite amusing as long as they're not about you. Don't e-mail it if you don't want the world to read it. If you anticipate that you may need to save an e-mail before finishing it, address it to yourself in case it's inadvertently sent.

- E-mail messages are forever.

You can't take it back. You may be able to erase your copy, but it most certainly will remain on the company's server—indefinitely.

- The delivery system doesn't diminish the importance of the quality of the message.

You still need to think, organize, write, revise, and make sure the tone is appropriate for your message and your audience. We haven't invented the technology to do the creating for us.

- The sheer volume of e-mail.

The average worker receives more than fifty e-mails every day. Many of us receive substantially more, and it's time consuming just to review them all. Set up filters in your e-mail client to organize and separate what's important from the personal mail that can wait. Then, instead of dealing with one inbox containing all your e-mails, you can select smaller folders based on priorities you've established.

You must discipline your use of e-mail or risk getting caught up in a time-gobbling, mind-numbing round of point-counterpoint dialogue. You may need to establish e-mail–free zones in your day, or to set regular periods when you will read and reply to your e-mails.

E-mail is a tool—and nothing more. Select it when it's the best method of communication in a given situation. There'll still be room for the confidential written memo, the formal business letter, the telephone call, and for the announcement tacked on the bulletin board.

CHAPTER 14

How to Control Paper Flow

Where does the time go?

You're spending from half to 70 percent of your working time dealing with paper—writing it, reading it, filing it, looking through it for another paper.

That's where the time goes.

The "paperless office," the idea that office automation would make physical paper documents redundant, was predicted by *BusinessWeek* as early as 1975. Yet, we can all agree that it's a myth; the use of e-mail alone in an organization causes an average 40 percent increase in paper consumption.

If you're ever going to get control of your time—which is to say your life—you're going to have to control the paper flood.

What to do? Here are ten suggestions to help manage paper flow.

10 WAYS TO REDUCE, CONTROL, AND ELIMINATE PAPER

1. Adopt a Constant Companion

Keep a notebook or planner with you all the time—in your attaché case, in your desk drawer, in your coat pocket or purse, on your night table. Capture those stray insights and write yourself reminders. This way you won't lose your ideas, and you won't have scraps of paper cluttering your life.

2. Manage Your Desktop(s)

A place for everything and everything in its place, on the actual desktop and the virtual one in the computer.

We're not talking neatness here. We're talking organization. Your desktop may extend to the floor and every other flat surface not already covered. But as long as you know where everything is and can lay your hands on it without having to wade through the stuff you don't want, you're in good shape.

Be honest with yourself, though. Do you *really* need all that stuff out in the open where you can see—and trip over—it? You may simply be worried that you'll lose it or forget to deal with it if you can't keep an eye on it. But careful organization and an accessible file cabinet will take care of that problem and help you clean up your working space, too.

3. Touch It Once

How many times do you pick up the same piece of paper, glance at it, scowl, and toss it back on the desk, promising yourself that you'll deal with it later?

Want to find out? Every time you handle a paper, slap a small sticker on it or make a pencil mark. After a week of this, gather up the clutter on your desk and count the stickers or marks.

Get the picture?

The first time you handle paper—from a one-page memo to a 500-page report—you should decide what to do with it. Then you should do it. Your choices are:

- Reroute (pass it on to someone else who should have it)
- Respond (then file it)
- Read (then file it)
- Recycle (as in, throw it in the recycle bin)

4. Exercise Good Sortsmanship

You should have three labeled stacking trays on your desk:

IN: This tray is for mail and memos when they first arrive. Leave the mail in this tray until you're ready to deal with it. Once you sort through the incoming mail, you'll make a decision about where it goes next. It never goes back in the IN tray.

OUT: The second tray is where you place outgoing mail— either external or internal mail to others within your office or building. You are done with whatever you put here.

TO FILE: The third tray is where you place items to be filed when you have time. Keep some file folders here so you can further organize each item. These folders should be labeled so they work best for you, but "Do," "Read," and "File" will work in 90 percent of cases. You will need to assign time to do your filing or other action so this tray does not get out of control.

Start by asking a variation on that fundamental question: Do I want or need to deal with this?

If not, does anybody need to?

If so, reroute and place it in the OUT box.

If not, it will go in the TO FILE box.

Do it now. Keep a supply of routing slips, interoffice mail envelopes, and whatever else you need to send the stuff on its way right away. And keep a bucket for recycling within easy reach.

For anything that makes it past this first cut, place each item in the proper folder in the TO FILE box. The "Do" folder carries with it a sense of urgency—this contains items that you're working on now. You can grab the "Read" folder on your way to lunch or a meeting. And items in the "File" folder will need to be filed by someone before it overflows.

5. Make It Disappear

There's only one thing better than getting rid of it as soon as you touch it, and that's never having to touch it at all.

Never automatically renew a subscription without balancing the periodical's worth to you with the time it takes to process it. Don't be shy about asking to be taken off mailing lists and routing slips.

For a wholesale purge of third-class mail, contact the Direct Marketing Association, DMA Consumer Assistance site at: *www. dmaconsumers.org.*

6. RSVP ASAP

If the paper needs only a brief response, do it right now. Create a speedy response:

- A personalized sticky note
- A note written on the bottom of the original letter or memo
- A half-sheet of business letterhead for a short note
- A phone call or e-mail if appropriate and more efficient

Are you being callous by sending the correspondent's own paper back to her? Not at all. Callous is putting off the response or not responding at all. You're being responsive and smart, and you're also saving paper.

7. File It and Forget It?

Do you really need to keep it?

Research shows that 80 percent of what we file away is never referenced again. Why take the time to file it now and to fumble over it dozens or even hundreds of times in the future if we don't really need it? Practice source-point pollution control.

If you do need to hang onto it, put it in the filing folder. Schedule a short filing session once a day (or week or month, depending on the volume of paper you're dealing with), for a time when you're not at your mental peak.

8. Strip, Clip, and Flip

If you receive trade publications on a regular basis, tear out the material you really need and toss the rest of the publication away. Be especially attentive to lists, tabulations, charts, and graphs that summarize a great deal of material in a small space. Think about how you might use this information and how you are going to find it later. Consider software made for this purpose if you reuse information with any frequency. Then recycle the rest.

While you're at it, toss out periodicals more than a year old, earlier drafts of written material, old reports that no longer have relevance. Schedule a brief session at the end of each week so the clutter level never gets unmanageable. While you're engaged in this relatively mindless work, you can decompress from a hard week of work, ease your transition into evening and weekend leisure time, and reflect on lessons learned.

9. Shift Gears When You Read

Reading everything at the same rate and in the same way makes as much sense as driving at the same speed on all roads and under all conditions.

You can skim some materials for main ideas, scan others for specific information, speed-read still others for the essence. A workshop or training session in speed reading would be time well spent if your job requires reading large amounts of material.

Save the material that requires time and concentration for your peak energy times and for times when you can concentrate without interruption. Reading difficult material requires your best effort, not the last shreds of consciousness at the end of the day.

10. The Tickler File

If you can adhere to the "touch it once" rule at all times, you'll save yourself tons of time.

If that rule's a little too rigid, create another file category, the tickler file.

Can't decide what to do with it? Not sure you should do anything at all? Put it in the tickler file. This file can become quite cumbersome; most advocates recommend a file for each day and another for each month. Put items in the appropriate file depending on when they need attention. Each day, attack the material in that day's file. If the amount of paper you are dealing with on a regular basis warrants this arrangement, go for it.

Alternatively, you can create a tickler system on your computer's or PDA's calendar. Just as you would enter a calendar item for a meeting, enter a reminder to work on a particular task. The reminder can be entered on any day or at repeating intervals to alert you to your tasks. The reminder can include phone numbers, the location of files, or any important information you'll need and are likely to forget—or don't want to remember.

Paper management will soon become a happy habit, one that will save you enormous amounts of time and remove a lot of the frustration from the workday.

CHAPTER 15

Turn Downtime into Productive Time

I f you were like most kids, you spent a lot of time waiting and wishing.

On Mondays, you'd start waiting and wishing for Fridays.

About the time you got to school each day, you'd start waiting and wishing for recess, and then lunch, and then the magic hour of 3:00, time to go home. How much time did you spend staring at the classroom clock, which moved impossibly slowly throughout the day and even slower as 3:00 approached?

Along about Halloween, you started waiting and wishing for Christmas. After Christmas, maybe you had a birthday to look forward to, otherwise there was baseball season, and once baseball season finally arrived, the wait for summer vacation would become all but intolerable.

After a few weeks of the endless, unstructured days of summer, you may have caught yourself feeling twinges of something that just might have been boredom. You might start wishing and waiting for your family's annual vacation, and long before you were ready, it was time to go back to school.

Then the cycle of waiting and wishing started all over again.

WHY DON'T ADULTS GET BORED?

It seemed like such a problem when you were a kid.

"Mom, I'm bored," you'd whine.

Mom would suggest a list of a dozen or so of your favorite activities, but you were tired of them all. She then might suggest that you kill a little time by working it to death mowing the lawn or cleaning your room or. . . .

Ah. Boredom isn't a lack of things to do, after all. It's a lack of anything you *want* to do. Boredom is equal parts restlessness (exhausted people don't get bored; they fall asleep) and lack of desire, complete disinterest in or aversion to any of the possible activities you might do next.

So, how come we never seem to get bored now?

We still get restless, although less frequently and intensely as we mature (read "become more frequently exhausted"). And we certainly continue to suffer from lack of desire (more or less frequently and intensely in inverse proportion to how much we genuinely enjoy our work and family life). But always we suffer, too, from too much to do and too little time to do it. We push on to the next task despite the lack of desire, full speed ahead.

Also, as we get older, we become aware of the dwindling number of days left to us. Time seems to speed up with great gobs of the stuff slipping away when we're not looking. Even the Mondays in February become more precious in that context, and we become loath to wish any of our time away.

What would you give for one of those endless Christmas Eve days of your youth, when time seemed to crawl and the hours refused to pass?

Fact is, you still have them, probably several little Christmas Eve days each working day. It's called waiting.

We wait for the coffee to perk, wait for the bus to come, wait for somebody to unjam the copy machine, wait for the client to respond to our voice mail message, wait for our luncheon date, wait in traffic, wait at the doctor's office or the Quicky Lube (which can never be quite Quicky enough). Time passes slowly at these times, not because we're anticipating the joy of good surprises under the Christmas tree, but because we've been displaced from our schedule and really should be somewhere else doing something different.

Most of us hate waiting. The more crowded your to-do list or day planner and the more impatient you tend to be, the more excruciating the waiting. We've reacted by trying to speed up our activity and eliminate the spaces between activities so we can cram more of them into a day.

THE WRONG WAY TO DO AWAY WITH WAITING

Folks who are always late never have to wait. They make everybody else wait. That's one solution to the problem of waiting.

In the world of academia, the amount of time students are allegedly required to wait for their teachers is a function of the teacher's position on the status pole. Teaching assistants and lecturers get little or no leeway. The untenured assistant prof gets less slack than the tenured associate professor colleague, and a student walks out of a tardy full professor's class at his or her peril unless at least 15 minutes have elapsed.

This scale is well known to many professors but virtually unknown to most students (who probably don't know their teacher's rank anyway).

But in most areas of life, relative status and power often dictate how long folks will wait for one another. Another determinant, of course, is dependency. You may not afford your plumber many status points, but you'll wait for him or her indefinitely as you keep swapping an empty bucket for a full one under the leaking water pipe. And maybe it's love or duty or just common sense, but we'll also wait indefinitely for a spouse or child every time.

How long are people required to wait for you? How long are they willing? What will they think of you while they wait?

Keeping people waiting probably isn't really your style anyway. Folks who seek help with time management are generally the ones being kept late by others. You get to places on time, and you expect others to do the same.

That's one reason why for you waiting is inevitable.

Elsewhere we've suggested that you build time cushions into your daily life. But when you allow more travel time than you might need under perfect circumstances and, by some miracle, circumstances actually turn out to be perfect, you'll show up places early. Good planning ensures even more waiting.

ONE WAY TO ELIMINATE SOME OF THE WAITING

Folks who keep you waiting tend to do so chronically. You can eliminate some of the waiting in your life by eliminating some of those people.

Stand me up once, shame on you. Stand me up twice, shame on me. I don't make a second appointment with the person who blew off the first one.

But we don't always have a choice. One of the chronic wait-creators in your life might be your boss, your spouse, or your kid. You can try to convert these folks into the cult of punctuality, but you'll most likely fail.

That's another reason why you'll have to wait sometimes.

MAKE THE WAIT MATTER LESS

You know certain activities will involve waiting. To the extent that it's in your power to do so, try to engage in those activities at times when waiting won't make as big a difference.

But few doctors schedule appointments for 6:00 (A.M. or P.M.) or Saturday afternoons. You have to take what you can get, including the cancellation at the dentist right in the middle of the day, just one more reason why . . .

YOU'LL ALWAYS HAVE TO WAIT

Three inescapable facts of modern life make waiting unavoidable.

- There are too many of us in the same place.
- We're all trying to get someplace else.
- We get in each other's way doing it.

No matter which line you pick at the grocery store, the line you pick will move the slowest, right? You'll always wind up behind the person with twenty-six items in the "12 Items or Less" line. That person will wait until those twenty-six items have been scanned and totaled before beginning to think about paying. And then the miscreant will drag out a change purse and pay in pennies, 4,284 of them.

What can you do? You can rant and bellow. You can make snide comments under your breath. You can dump your groceries on the ground and walk away. You can switch to another line—and wind up behind someone who wants to get a refund on a quart of ice cream purchased at another store, in another decade.

Or you can take what seems to be a lemon and make lemonade.

HOW TO USE THE WAIT TIME: THREE STEPS THAT WILL MAKE YOU MORE PRODUCTIVE AND LESS STRESSED

Step 1. Accept the Wait as Inevitable

Waiting is destructive for two reasons. First, if you haven't allowed sufficient time for waiting, the wait will destroy your schedule and cause you to be late for other appointments and to fail to complete necessary tasks. You can defuse this time bomb, lowering the stakes in the waiting game, by refusing to overpack the schedule. That way, the wait can't hurt you as much.

But waiting can be even more destructive because of what it does to your insides. Oh, how we seethe as we idle in traffic or jiggle and fidget in the waiting room. That seething can trigger a corrosive stress reaction, harming us physically as well as emotionally.

You may not be able to eliminate the wait, but you can minimize the damage it can do to you by accepting what you can't change. Stop blaming the fates (or the jerk who kept you waiting). Stop festering about where you should be and what you should be doing. Be where you are, doing what you're doing.

Achieving the acceptance mind-state is not easy, and absolutely impossible for some people. No matter how often they tell themselves, in good faith, that they cannot control the situation and to make the best of it, these types will continue to rage and stress. So, try this technique and see if you're susceptible to reason. You may be pleasantly surprised, as will all others with you.

Step 2. Rename the Wait

You speed through the day, pushing your body and mind beyond fatigue, putting off needed rest . . .

- until you get home and can finally kick off your shoes and put your feet up, or
- until the kids are fed and bathed and storied and put to bed, or
- until the weekend, or
- until the vacation, or
- until retirement, or . . .

Some of those "untils" never come, of course. And sometimes when they do, they come too late to help, because you've already been pushed past the point where you *can* relax.

Meanwhile, you may have rushed and squirmed and fretted your way through four or five potential rest periods a day.

Rename the wait. Call it a rest instead.

Oh, what a difference. Waits are cold frustrations. Rests are warm comforts.

Could you really feel warm and embraced stuck in the middle of traffic? Probably not right away. Such a major change in mind-set takes some working at and some getting used to. But it can be done. Anger and frustration are not inevitable results of waiting.

Step 3. Use the Wait

You're running late, racing the green turn arrow to the intersection. But the bozo in front of you is poking along, blissfully unaware of your need to make that signal. The bozo, of course, makes the light while causing you to miss it. It's just one of the unwritten laws of physics.

You can scream and fume, spiking your blood pressure while adrenaline oozes out your ears. Or you can proclaim a rest and take one of your mini-vacations for deep breathing or mental roaming.

Too unproductive for you? Spend forty-five seconds visualizing a perfect golf swing or tennis stroke. (There's evidence that positive visualization might even improve your stroke or swing.)

Conduct a mental dialogue with someone you've always wanted to talk to.

Brainstorm solutions to a problem.

Plan a week's worth of dinner menus.

You'll wait a lot longer than forty-five seconds at the doctor's office. So come prepared. Bring that book you've been trying to find time to read, your "read" folder from work, or the crossword puzzle you'll never have time for later.

Tend to your knitting.

Write a haiku.

Read one of those moldy magazines that seem to survive only in historical societies and waiting rooms. Pick something you wouldn't usually read. You'll gain a new perspective on life and learn things you never would have known. And that way it won't make any difference that the magazine is old; it's all new to you anyway.

RESULTS OF TURNING THE WAIT INTO A REST

You'll be better rested and more relaxed (and better read).

You'll be more efficient and effective.

Who knows? You might write some great haiku.

And you'll get to where you were going at exactly the same time you would have anyway.

CHAPTER 16

Procrastination

N o time management technique will do you any good if you still allow yourself to postpone the difficult or the unpleasant. The job doesn't get any less unpleasant while you wait. Quite the contrary, your sense of dread will build, making it increasingly difficult to bring yourself to the task.

And it won't get any easier, either. Rather, your delay will merely complicate matters. You'll have to deal with the complications, often before you can even get at the original job.

Thus, procrastination costs time while creating unnecessary stress.

Procrastination is the thief of time.
—Edward Young (1683–1765)

So, if it's so awful, why do so many of us procrastinate? Why are there some jobs we just never seem to "get around to," despite the consequences of our evasion?

SIX REASONS WHY WE PROCRASTINATE AND SIX STRATEGIES TO PUT OFF PUTTING OFF

Reason 1. You Haven't Really Committed to Doing the Job

If you were to attend a workshop for would-be and beginning novelists and ask them why they want to write a novel, a project that demands a huge commitment of time, energy, and emotion, most of the answers would fall into one of three categories.

The first reason, simply stated, is that the writer feels good while writing (or, conversely, feels wretched when denied the opportunity to write). For some, writing seems to be almost an addiction or a compulsion, although a relatively harmless one as addictions go.

The second set of reasons basically cluster around the notion of communication and storytelling: "I have something to say, and a novel seems to be the best way to say it," or "I've got a story I want or need to tell." Some folks even say that the story seems to be using them to get itself told.

The third set of reasons stems from the notion, sadly mistaken, that novelists become rich and famous with relatively little effort. Many of the folks in this group don't want to write a novel; they want to have written a novel, so they can reap the supposed rewards.

Most of the folks in the first category and many in the second actually go on to write that novel. Few in the third group ever do.

Occasionally you would hear a reason that doesn't fall into any of these categories.

"My English teacher back in good old P.S. 134 said I'd make a good novelist," one might say, or "Folks in my book group think my life story would be inspirational."

Assuming that they aren't being coy, that they don't really mean "I think I'd make a great novelist," or "I think my life story would be inspirational," an appropriate response to this sort of reason borders on Mom's old admonition: "If somebody told you to jump off a cliff, would you do it?"

The key here is the source of the motivation. We generally don't need to force or trick ourselves into performing actions that are internally motivated. But the more the motivation comes from the English teacher or the book club or the mate or the boss or any other external source, the less likely we are to do it.

Know anybody who got into the family bakery business, or became a lawyer, or joined the Marines because somebody expected or demanded it? If so, you probably know an unhappy baker or lawyer or Marine.

You may chronically put off an activity because you aren't really sold on doing it at all. Reasons include:

- You don't think it's your job.
- You think it's somebody else's job.
- The job's a waste of time.
- You have important things to do.

If that's the case, you need to answer two fundamental questions:

1. What's in it for me if I do it?
2. What will happen to me if I don't?

The first question may redirect and increase your motivation. You're no longer doing it because someone said you ought to. You're doing it to impress a boss, help a friend, make money, or get to a task you really enjoy.

The second question is the negative of the first. Your motivation may become avoidance of something unpleasant, like a lousy job evaluation, an angry, alienated spouse, or a disappointed child, for example.

If you can find no internal motivation—no benefit for doing the job and no penalty for not doing it, you may well decide not to do it at all. It's not one of your priorities, and you probably shouldn't be doing it.

Even if you can see a benefit to doing the job, you may still decide that the costs in time and energy (and the other things you aren't doing) outweigh the benefits. In that case you can:

1. Do what you have to do to get out of the job. That's not the same thing as simply putting it off. This is an active, conscious decision not to do it and to accept the consequences, if any. In the long run, that sort of decision costs less, in time and stress, than does the passive resistance

of procrastination. You will feel relief when the job is no longer hanging over your head.

Or

2. Do it anyway—but for your own reasons.

Reason 2. You're Afraid of the Job

This is a hard thing for many of us to admit—to ourselves let alone to someone else. But it may be what's keeping you from doing a job you need and want to accomplish. If you can identify your reluctance as fear or low self-esteem and track it to its source, you can deal with the fear and get on with the job. Here are three of the most common varieties of performance anxiety:

1. Fear of failure

Consider the student who never studies and flunks out. He can always tell himself, "If I had studied, I would have passed the stupid course." But what if he had studied—and still failed?

For most of us, "won't" is a lot easier to deal with than "can't." If you don't try it, you don't have to confront the possibility that you can't do it. You will always be able to tell yourself and others that you could have been a great success at just about anything you wanted to do.

2. Fear of success

On the other hand, if you do pass the course, folks will expect you to do it again, or to go out and get a job, or to apply what you've learned. If you never try, you'll never have to face the consequences of success, either.

3. Fear of finishing

"If I pass the course, I'll graduate. If I graduate, I'll . . ."

You'll what?

If you don't pass the course, you'll never have to find out what happens next.

If you never write the novel, you'll never have to know whether a publisher would have accepted it.

If you don't finish basic training, you'll never have to know whether you could have really hacked it in the military.

Sometimes the not knowing seems more acceptable than the possible consequences of finding out for sure.

But how sad to let such fears prevent you from even trying.

Identify the fear or the issue that has caused your low self-esteem. Give it a name and confront it. Imagine the consequences of your actions or non-actions as objectively as you can.

The fear won't go away. But if the goal is worth pursuing, and you set your sights on the benefits of reaching the goal, you'll be able to act despite the fear.

Reason 3. You Don't Place a High Enough Priority on the Activity

You're sold on the idea that somebody ought to do the task. You'll even agree, if pressed, that you're the person to do it. You may even want to do it.

You just don't want or need to do it enough, and you always want or need to do something else more.

Thus, the poor task—cleaning the leaves out of the rain gutters in autumn, to cite one mundane example—keeps getting bumped down the list, below other, more pressing jobs. You've got to go grocery shopping first, because you won't have anything to eat if you don't. You've got to mow the lawn first, because it will look awful if you don't. (And nobody can see the leaves in the rain gutters, after all.)

This sort of procrastination problem may eventually work itself out. As the other tasks get done, those leafy gutters work their way up the list. Or the problem may take on a higher priority after the first hard rain of the season.

Establishing priorities is subjective, especially when dealing with activities that are neither urgent nor particularly important relative to other activities. Take a look at the job that just isn't getting done and see if you can redefine it in terms of the ultimate benefit you'll receive for doing it.

First time through this definition may be negative:

"If I don't clean out the rain gutters, I'll get a flood in the garden the first time it rains hard."

Positive motivations tend to be much stronger. Recast it in the positive form:

"If I clean out the rain gutters, I'll protect my garden from flooding."

Is that important to you?

Are there other ancillary benefits to getting the task done?

- "I'll finally stop worrying about it."
- "I'll get some nice exercise out in the sunshine."
- "I can listen to music while I work."

Are these considerations enough to move the task up the list? If so, get at it! But if not, you must either resign yourself to living with the consequences of your nonaction or find a way to get the job done without actually having to do it. You could hire the neighbor kid, thus trading money for time, for example. Or, you could add "It won't cost anything if I do it myself" to your list of ancillary benefits, perhaps tipping the balance in favor of doing it.

Reason 4: You Don't Know Enough to Do the Task

When a writer gets "writer's block," it's often the subconscious mind's helpful way of suggesting that he doesn't really know what the hell he's talking about.

This is true for other sorts of motivational blocks as well. You may simply not know enough to do the job properly. You haven't consciously recognized or admitted this to yourself, but you know it deep down, and this knowledge is manifesting itself in strong aversion.

Gather the information you need. Look at the job as a series of smaller tasks that aren't as intimidating. If all else fails, read the directions (a desperate last resort for many of us). Then plunge into the task.

Learn to discern between the legitimate need to gather information and a stalling mechanism whereby reading the book or going to talk to the guy at the hardware store is simply a way to put off confronting the job. If your problem is "lack of desire" rather than lack of information, you'll need a different strategy, namely, what to do when . . .

Reason 5. You Just Plain Don't Want To!

On a preference scale of 1 to 10, giving Rover his flea bath rates a minus 2.

It isn't merely unpleasant. It isn't just disgusting. It's downright dangerous. Rover does not like his flea bath. Last time you tried this little experiment in torture, you wound up scratched, Rover was traumatized, and the bathroom looked like a tidal wave had hit it.

The fleas are back. Rover is scratching. If you don't do something—and fast—you'll have fleas all over the house.

You've got two choices, and you don't need a book on time management to tell you what they are:

1. Gut it out, or
2. Farm it out.

Get on the old raincoat, put a tarp down around the tub, and pop Rover into the suds. Or make an appointment with your friendly neighborhood dog groomer.

Reason 6. You Find It Difficult to Concentrate

You may think about what you're going to cook for dinner tonight or you daydream about what you're going to do this weekend. You may be distracted by ringing telephones or other people's conversations, or you may spend time performing such mindless tasks as reorganizing your desk drawer or making lots of unnecessary trips to the restroom or copy room. So you put off getting the job done; you sit and think about it but take no action.

Take the initiative to confront this concentration problem. If it's serious and constant, you may benefit from professional help. If you're not ready to admit that it's out of your control, then plan alternatives for occasional lapses of concentration. Stand and stretch, or get a few minutes of fresh air (set yourself a limit—this is just a break, after all). Change a distracting work environment by moving your desk or computer, or place a barrier to block your view. Take away the temptation to wander away from your work area by making sure you have the supplies and information you need before starting on a task. Set a timed reminder to help you stay on task. By acknowledging this "weakness," you can modify your behavior accordingly.

THE MAGIC BULLET FOR PROCRASTINATION

There isn't one, sorry. But there is a solution if you're willing to, as Nike advises, "just do it."

Identify the reason for the procrastination. Don't try to be perfect. Confront your attitudes and fears. Weigh the consequences. Break down the big intimidating projects into small approachable tasks. Give yourself thirty minutes to finish each one. Then deal with it!

CHAPTER 17

Time Management for Students

F ull-time and part-time students face unique time management issues, as well as experiencing concerns common to most people with busy schedules. We present some tips that students can use to better manage their time.

PRINCIPLES OF TIME MANAGEMENT FOR STUDENTS

1. Every individual performs better at certain times of the day. You should use these periods when you are able to concentrate more fully as study times for your hardest classes, rather than errands or relaxing. It may require experimentation to determine when your best time(s) occur unless you already know that you're a "morning person" or "night person."
2. Tackle difficult subjects before the easier or more enjoyable ones. Work on one subject at a time for maximum focus.
3. Try studying in short time blocks divided by short breaks. You'll tire less easily and your brain will continue to process information during the breaks.
4. Pick a study area and always use it exclusively for studying. This trains your mind to accomplish what you want to with minimal "start up." The area should be comfortable (but not too comfortable), quiet, have good lighting, and low traffic or other distractions. Your bed, by the way, is for sleeping.
5. Use down time effectively. Have index cards with formulas or anything you need to memorize, so that you can study

them while doing laundry, between classes, or waiting in line. This works well for material that exists in discrete units and requires significant review before it's absorbed. Audio material can be reviewed while on the bus or walking to class. Always carry a book wherever you go in case of unforeseen delays in traffic, at airports, etc.

6. Don't forget to sleep and eat properly. It's easy to sacrifice your sleep, and you may not miss it until you crash. There will be times you need to pull an all-nighter, but making the effort to get a regular night's sleep on a regular basis will make you much more effective during waking hours. Your health is important; eat in balance to maintain it properly.

7. If your mind tends to wander while you're trying to study, keep a notepad with you to record your thoughts. This will clear your mind so you can refocus on your studies. If a particular problem won't go away, develop a quick, mini-plan for dealing with it complete with steps and schedule. Write it down, then go back to the books. (Like an extra book, it's a good idea to keep a notepad or notebook with you all the time to catch stray thoughts and ideas, both brilliant and mundane.)

8. Respect your study time and encourage others to respect it as well. You need to be left alone during these times even if your roommates or classmates feel like partying. This includes telephone interruptions as well. Turn off the phone if you need to. Enforcing time for study will require tact, resolve, and maturity.

9. All work and no play makes the student a dull person. The college student should carve out time to experience social life as well as the academic. All students, even part timers, can benefit from sharing thoughts and opinions with their classmates. Good time management will permit a balance of activities.

10. Plan your day. Know each morning where you need to go and what you need to accomplish that day. Bring with

you what you'll use that day, including lunch, so you don't waste time later.

11. Reward yourself when you meet your goals. The rewards can be no more than an extra five minutes of break time, but they support behaviors you're trying to adopt, and even minor bonuses will be positive and worthwhile reinforcements.

12. You've had a busy day and are exhausted looking at another busy day tomorrow. Before cashing in, do one more task, even if it's just looking at a page of notes for 30 seconds. You'll have a greater sense of accomplishment for the day that you'll carry forward to tomorrow.

13. If you're having trouble with a particular class, with study skills, or some other problem, seek out assistance as soon as possible before the issue gets out of control. Colleges want their students to succeed and most have extensive support systems available for the asking. Don't waste your time struggling with a problem alone.

14. Class time is important, obviously. Make sure you use it effectively by being alert, prepared, ready to absorb as much as possible. You are doing yourself a disservice by attending class when you're too tired or hungover to concentrate. It's better to sleep in, borrow a classmate's notes later, and promise yourself not to miss another class.

Undoubtedly, you are already practicing some of these techniques, and have tried and discarded others. Try those that are new to you to determine if they're beneficial. They can not only help you to use your time more effectively, but will also improve your educational experience.

CHAPTER 18

Time Management for Project Management

P roper time management techniques are essential to good project management. In fact, project management considers time an important resource, and the timing of activities essential to achieving the project's goals. This and the fact that so many workers are responsible for projects makes it valuable to consider how time and project management are interrelated. Those interested in improving their time management skills can benefit greatly from learning the principles of project management. And whether you are the project manager or project team member, you should take the responsibility to understand and do your best to follow these principles.

WHERE TO START

A project starts with a specification. This is the definition of the project and includes, at the very least, a statement of the problem that the project hopes to solve. The wise project manager knows that the specification contains errors, ambiguities, and misdirections. Depending on the complexity of the project, the specification will change many times before the project is completed, and probably with increasing frequency as the deadline draws closer. Everyone who was involved in the creation of the specification or who will use the specification knows this, but will embrace some of its inaccuracies to the bitter end, fighting for the errors of his choice. One part of the specification that will not change, even if it's completely arbitrary, is the due date.

The project manager must call meetings, assemble all the project stakeholders, and review the specification point by point until everyone has the same understanding (and it's in writing) of what is required, when it's required, and the cost. The time and effort spent in this initial step of project definition will save time later, and will protect careers. The project demands this effort and the project team deserves it.

A complex project may take months to complete, involve hundreds of people, dozens of suppliers, and has the potential to make or break an organization. So, spending time on getting it right the first time is understandable. But minor projects or tasks so small that they can't even be termed "projects," can and will benefit from the same initial definition step. If you or your team is responsible for a task and you don't have a clear idea of what your goal looks like, then you are doomed. You can go through all of the rest of the steps to reach your goal, but may miss it by a mile. At this stage you should look at:

- The big picture. Does this project make sense, and will the parts work when they're put together?
- Teams. If the project requires a team and particularly if it requires more than one, how will team members work together, communicate, divide or share responsibilities?
- Time. You have an end date, but the individual steps required have their own schedules. Are they achievable?
- Costs. Budgets are great until you exceed one, then various people become agitated to various degrees. Build in a cushion, the largest one you can get away with.
- Human resources. Teams can consist of consultants, hired help, freelancers, vendors, and others. They all need to play by the same game plan and be committed for the project to work.
- Other resources. Any materials and equipment necessary to do the work needs to be specified. If new software is required, for example, it will need to be purchased, installed, and may require training. Check that costs have been correctly estimated and time built in so the team is not expected to be using software before it has learned how, or hardware before it's installed.

Note, as mentioned above, that specifications will change. Someone will come up with a new idea, stroll into your office, and ask the innocent question: "Wouldn't it be great if the project included. . . ." He or she will then proceed to describe a fabulous new feature or function that the original specification overlooked. Perhaps it would be great if the project included that feature or function. You may be as excited as your visitor about this idea and want to see it implemented in the worst way. Okay. Call the stakeholders, discuss and agree upon the change and its repercussions to the big picture, the team, time needed, additional resources needed, and costs. Get it in writing.

All of this may seem like a lot of work; it is. Invest the time up front. Look before you leap. You and the team will be glad later.

BUILDING A PROJECT FRAMEWORK

The next step in managing a project is determining what you actually need to do and how to do it. This is done by converting the specification into a set of tasks or activities. The activities need to be simple enough that they can be managed, linked to each other logically, and ordered. For simple projects, there may be only a few straightforward steps; for large projects, the steps may need to be broken down several times and the linking can become complex. The steps are descriptions in themselves, with instructions for the person who will be doing the work, and an estimate of the time involved.

This part of the planning process involves careful time management. Some steps can take place independently of others, but many will be linear and require one step to be completed before the next can begin. The same can be said of many tasks we undertake every day; we just are less formal in organizing them. We need to drop off the dry cleaning before we can pick it up, of course, and we may need to research information before we write a report. If we stopped to consider how much time it will take to perform the research, we would have a better idea of how long it will take to produce the report.

TASK ALLOCATION

The next stage is allocating the steps of the project to individuals in the project team. This often requires a global view; the manager needs to be aware of outside demands on team members, and most importantly, to take advantage of individual strengths and build skills within the team for future projects. Tasks can be modified to fit the experience of individuals, and grouped if they have common requirements. Task allocation is an opportunity to develop the team as a collection of individuals.

Time management is task management, whether for a project or for your own individual tasks. By thoroughly understanding a task, you can allocate the appropriate resources and schedule it accurately. If you are working with your own personal set of skills, you should be realistic in understanding how to take advantage of your strengths and accommodate your weaknesses to accomplish your goals.

TIME ESTIMATING

We've already seen how by breaking down a project into manageable steps, it's possible to assign them a schedule. Then, by putting together the steps into the longest path, you can get a good idea of the total time the project will require. There are lots of assumptions to be made and time estimating can be a scary process. It's important to keep records of how long individual activities take so you can use this experience in future projects.

If you don't have the results of previous projects to use in estimating the current one, then you're left with trying to guess time requirements as accurately as possible. It's tempting to be optimistic, ignoring potential or unknown problems, and assuming things will go smoothly. Problems have been known to occur in the best planned project, so it's wise to build in some slack so it doesn't blow your schedule out of the water. Your superiors may encourage you to deliver faster, and there may be honest business reasons to do so, but resist the pressure to compromise quality or give unrealistic promises.

These principles apply equally to planning individual tasks. To successfully work your way through the day's to-do list, you need to know how much time each task will require, and be realistic in establishing your schedule. No matter how urgent they may be, or strong your desire to cross them off your list, you will not complete five three-hour tasks in an eight-hour day.

MANAGING THE PROJECT

Once the specifying, planning, task allocation, and time estimating is completed, its time to pull the trigger on your project. It will be necessary to apply controls to the project, despite its apparent willingness to take on a life of its own. Because you have created steps or stages for a complex project, you know what needs to be accomplished and by what date. These milestones enable you to monitor progress (forming the basis for the popular "progress report") and serve as interim goals for the individuals or groups working assigned to them. Sometimes it's preferable to establish milestones that don't match the steps of the project, but recognize a particular achievement resulting from the completion of several steps.

Effective communication is a critical component of project management; it merits its own set of rules. The team must communicate with each other and their manager; if there are multiple teams, they must communicate with each other; and the project manager must communicate with senior management. Communications permit you to monitor and report progress, encourage cooperation, and motivate. Any breakdown in communications within the project management team can spell disaster.

Monitoring progress through milestones, particularly tasks with multiple steps, is an equally effective technique on a personal level. And as we've seen in the chapter on communications, your ability to communicate can be decisive in completing tasks.

QUALITY CONTROL

Depending on what the deliverable for the project is, some level of testing and quality control is typically involved during the project's life. If it's necessary, it should be planned for and scheduled as a part of the product's development. A proper specification will include the level of quality required.

You apply quality control to your own work, although typically it's an unconscious reflex. When you hand in a report, for example, you'll feel a certain sense of satisfaction based on its quality. If it was a rush job, you may feel relief that you made the deadline. If it represented your best work with quality research, lucid writing, and insightful conclusions, then you'll have a justified sense of pride. Different tasks require different levels of effort, and understanding this is an important lesson to learn.

SUMMARY

We haven't attempted to document all the steps of project management, but have tried to point out significant components and how they parallel management and particularly time management for the individual. Project management is an art and a science, but its principles, as we've seen, can apply beyond their formal application.

Project management provides opportunities and pitfalls that working solo can't. Whatever the outcome, it is always a learning experience for those involved in the project. It should be clear that better understanding of expectations and processes, greater cooperation and communication, additional commitment to the outcome, greater utility of resources, and of course, superior time management—signal better project management and better results.

CHAPTER 19

Time Management Software

M any software programs currently are available to improve the individual's and organization's efficiency over a broad range of tasks. These programs can, for example, maintain a calendar of meetings and appointments as well as a to-do list, keep group contact lists, manage e-mail, make and file notes, and help manage projects. The "smarter" applications link functions so that data needs to be updated in one place only, and the update will flow to all connected sites.

Some programs are designed specifically to help work groups collaborate and communicate more effectively. By making schedules of each individual available to all via a web-based program, for example, the task of scheduling meetings is greatly simplified, particularly when members are scattered in different locations. Address book contacts can also be shared by a group. Still other software applications address enterprise-wide productivity issues by attempting to help users organize the creative and innovation process, promote brainstorming, capture ideas, encourage strategic thinking and planning, and automate business processes. The postmortem process can also be greatly simplified due to the built-in reporting and analysis capabilities of many project management programs. Organization intranets are now incorporating collaboration functionality to facilitate teamwork, as are client-based applications (Microsoft Office updates, for example, will include more collaboration functionality allowing users to write, edit, and share documents remotely).

Capitalizing on the proliferation of personal digital assistants, new software packages ensure that all the devices an individual may use whether in the office, at home, or on the road, are synchronized. Many programs allow export and import of data so that other users can share and use information in other programs. Many programs are designed to work in conjunction with common information management and/or e-mail applications.

THE FUTURE IS HERE

There are software applications available to facilitate almost any time management need and shorten almost any process. All promise to save time through the use of computers' technological advantages: storage, sorting, linking, and conversion. Enter contact information once, for example, and it becomes available indefinitely, is readily updated, and can be accessed and transferred easily to other applications, devices, and users.

Yet, time management software, while providing distinct advantages over paper-based systems, is just an improved tool in the hands of the user. Much as an electric saw cuts faster than a hand saw, time management software will improve work flow compared with a system based on note cards or notebooks, and written lists. And because so many projects involve team members working in different locations, a shared project management program is essential to coordinate their efforts.

Time management software can provide definite productivity gains if:

- The installation and configuration stages are properly managed
- Initial data entry is not excessively time consuming
- Updating and maintenance of data is convenient
- The learning curve for new users is not overly steep
- The software is stable and available; crashes are infrequent
- Users consider the output valuable

A complete description of all time management software packages available is beyond the scope of this book. And, because programs come and go with significant frequency, any list will become quickly outdated. We won't consider browser, e-mail packages, or search engines here.

Here are some examples of categories and typical applications. Note that many fine and appropriate software packages are not included, and those that do make the list are not meant as recommendations.

PROJECT MANAGEMENT SOFTWARE

For any project that involves multiple participants, multiple steps, or the necessity to capture time for billing purposes, project management software offers distinct time-saving advantages. These programs permit individual users to establish to-do tasks for themselves, others, and groups, and track completion against schedule or forecast. They offer the capacity to track multiple projects. Some examples include:

Microsoft Project (Microsoft) integrates with Microsoft Office XP and Vista, so it lets Office regulars get up and running with relative ease in an application that would otherwise require training. Managers who don't use Office may prefer a package specific to their businesses, such as construction, sales, or manufacturing.

FastTrack Schedule (AEC Software, Inc.) is a project management tool that breaks down projects in terms of human, financial, and time resources needed to complete different stages. FastTrack will alert users to planning conflicts and has templates to help load data for new projects. Its dynamic nature accommodates changes in resource availability.

OrgPlus Professional (HumanConcepts) is basically an application for organizational charting; it also permits the building of what-if business scenarios for use in HR decision making.

SureTrak Project Manager 3.0 and Primavera (Primavera Systems, Inc.) are project management software programs.

Merlin (Project Wizard) is project management software that also functions as a content-management system to keep versions of documents, list authors, and share them with team members.

OmniPlan (The Omni Group) is a simple, Mac-only project management application.

Daylite (Marketcircle) is a project planning and tracking program that allows members of a workgroup to share information such as sales-call reports or project schedules. By defining recurring projects with standard steps, Daylite will generate due dates for each step automatically.

INFORMATION CAPTURE, SHARING, AND DEVELOPMENT SOFTWARE

The following programs help with idea management:

MindManager (Mindjet) has more than 70 percent of the PC-based market (and more of the enterprise market) for mind mapping software, which allows the user to capture, organize, and share information. A means to organize ideas (you start with a topic and add branches as you mine your idea)—its integration with FastTrack project management software allows those ideas to be incorporated into a project management framework. MindManager can assign ideas to a specific individual and show completion.

Visual Mind (Mind Technologies) is a graphical planning and organizing application.

EMC Documentum (EMC Corporation) permits the capture, management, delivery, and archiving of documents used in invoice processing, claims handling, loan processing, and applications processing.

OneNote 2007 (Microsoft) is a note-taking and information-management program.

COLLABORATION SOFTWARE

These programs allow you and your colleagues to stay on the same page:

Lotus Notes (IBM) offers e-mail, instant messaging, notebook, calendar/resources reservation, and means to interact with collaborative applications.

Basecamp (37 Signals) is a Web-based application that facilitates real-time group decision making.

FacilitatePro (Facilitate.com) is a Web-based brainstorming and decision-making tool.

PERSONAL ORGANIZATION SOFTWARE AND TO-DO LIST MANAGERS

The following programs will help you stay organized:

Calendar Creator (Encore Software Inc.) uses templates of daily planners, weekly organizers, monthly and yearly calendars (including Franklin Covey® layouts) to create a personal calendar.

TreePad (Freebyte) is a personal information manager, organizer, database, and word processor. It stores notes, documents, hyperlinks, and images and makes them easily accessible.

CHAPTER 20

Just Don't Do It!

Much of time management seeks to help us do things faster and do more than one thing at once, so we can fit more doing into the same limited amount of time.

But no time management plan can work without attention to the tasks themselves.

Here's where the famous admonition to "work smarter, not harder" comes into play.

Spend just a little time today questioning some of the tasks you do every day, and you can save tons of time every day from now on.

HOW TO ELIMINATE UNNECESSARY STEPS

"I'm so busy doing the dance," a worker laments, "I haven't got time to learn the steps."

Let's free up some time by eliminating some of those steps, the ones that aren't getting you anywhere.

Get Rid of the Paperwork Morgue

For those of you who work in government agencies, or other large bureaucracies, you may be acquainted with the emphasis on paperwork and procedures. Certainly, procedures can be worthwhile; they permit many things to happen that we want to happen and prevent some of those that shouldn't. Paperwork, too, is useful when backup is required. But we're talking here about large amounts of unnecessary paperwork and pointless procedures.

Paperwork and procedures create work for some people, and are therefore valuable to those people. They see and will always see the importance of completing all the paperwork, and of following the procedures. That's the way it's been done, possibly for years or even generations.

The general trend to digitize documents so they can be stored and accessed is slowly overcoming the death grip of the paper bureaucracy, but these folks are not going down without a fight.

If you find yourself engaged in completing, filing, sorting, searching for, or trying to find room for paperwork that serves no purpose other than providing work for someone else, then perhaps you should seek an alternative. If you follow procedures and fill out forms that are destined to be sent to a morgue where they will never again see the light of day, you have an obligation to try to change the procedures that are wasting your time.

Are a couple of unnecessary forms and an extra step in filing really worth the fight it takes to get rid of them? Depends on how many people you have to fight and how hard you have to fight them. But you *do* have the power to stem some of your daily work flood. You don't need status or tenure if you have common sense and the voice of reason on your side. Couch your proposal in terms of the good of the organization, to achieve the goals you and your boss share, and you have a chance to succeed.

It *is* worth it. It's worth questioning the need for any process that requires your time and attention. Get rid of it now and you draw the benefits every day from now on.

TWO MORE FORMS OF UNNECESSARY WORK—BUSY WORK AND WORK AVOIDANCE WORK

In a lot of office settings bosses create busy work for subordinates rather than have to face the prospect of figuring out something real for them to do (or to endure watching them play computer solitaire).

You may also have caught yourself creating busy work for yourself because it makes you feel productive. Also, doing something simple but unnecessary may be a lot easier than actually planning what you ought to be doing next.

When you take a hard look at the things you do, don't just look to eliminate tasks that others ask or require you to do. Get rid of the self-generated busy work, too.

You may have caught yourself doing low-priority or unnecessary jobs to avoid doing the harder task you really need to be doing. For me, almost anything is easier than organizing a long, complex piece of writing or engaging in budget planning. It's amazing what I'll do to avoid these. And as long as I'm doing something, I'm just "too busy" to get to the onerous stuff.

In many offices today, the most pervasive form of work avoidance work is "surfing" the net. Web casting certainly keeps you busy, you're undoubtedly learning something (although its application to the workplace may be tenuous), and once you learn to find your way around you start having a wonderful time.

But that seductive screen gobbles time in huge gulps. And while you're "busy" surfing, other work is waiting—work that may put you under severe time pressure later.

Not all net surfing is work avoidance, of course (just as not all sidewalk sweeping is done merely in the cause of looking busy). But the surfer knows how to determine the usefulness of the ride.

When you catch yourself doing work avoidance work, redirect your time and energy.

THE "NOT-TO-DO" LIST AND THE "LET-OTHERS-DO-IT" LIST

We do a lot of what we do today because we did it yesterday, and the day before. We're accustomed to doing it, perhaps even in the habit of doing it, and doing it is actually easier than not doing it.

You may need to create a *"not-to-do"* list to remind you of the tasks you've decided to eliminate from your routine. This may seem silly, but that doesn't necessarily mean it's a bad idea. See if the list helps you; just don't let anybody else see it.

Which leads us to those tasks that should be done—but not by *you*.

Make a list of those tasks you now perform but which you feel should be done by someone else. Reasons for putting tasks on this list include:

- I lack the authority to do it right.
- I lack the skill, information, or tools to do it right.
- If I do it, other tasks with higher priorities don't get done.

This list does not, unfortunately, include:

- "I don't want to," or
- "I don't like to," or even
- "It's not in my job description" (although this point probably should become the subject of a future planning discussion with your supervisor).

DELEGATING, SWAPPING, AND LETTING GO

Once you determine that someone else should be doing a job you're now performing, you have three options for getting someone else to do it.

1. Delegating

A lot of folks are fortunate enough to have someone else to answer the phone for them, thus absorbing the interruptions and, of course, screening callers. Some folks have other folks to open and sort their mail for them, too, and make the coffee, and fill out all those stupid forms and a lot of other less-than-glamorous tasks.

Time management books always suggest that we save time by delegating such jobs to others. (Note that this doesn't actually "save" any time. It simply shifts the time from one person to another.)

Unfortunately, this option is open only to bosses. If you have no one to boss, you have to answer your own phone and open your own mail. This time management book is for you, too, so let's explore two other options.

2. Swapping

One program assistant loves to file and fill out forms but dreads answering the telephone. (I believe that phonephobia is much more prevalent in the workplace than any of us would like to admit.)

Another program assistant, working in the same office, hates the paperwork but loves answering the phone.

Not surprisingly, the first assistant doesn't do a very good job with callers, while the second is invariably courteous, cheerful, and helpful.

Neither assistant has the authority to delegate work to the other. But they might be able to arrange a trade, with their supervisor's approval, of course.

3. Letting Go

Some folks don't let anyone else open their mail or answer their telephone because they won't, rather than because they can't.

This may stem from a lack of trust in the subordinate, of course—a bad situation for a variety of reasons, but the inability to let go may not have anything to do with anybody else. Some folks just have a terrible time delegating. Even if they do assign a task to someone else, they find themselves "supervising" so much, they wind up spending as much or more time on it—and alienating the coworker in the process.

When you hand a job off to someone else, don't tie a string to it. Make sure your coworkers know what they're supposed to accomplish, and then let them accomplish it their way. If they don't get the desired results in the allotted time, work on these specific outcomes. But keep your hands off the work in progress.

That way you really save the time, and your coworker doesn't have to put up with your fussing.

DO IT NOW, DO IT LATER, OR DO IT NEVER

Does it need a meeting, or will a memo do? Does it need a memo, or will a phone call do? Does it need a phone call? Does it need doing at all?

"Because we've always done it" is a rotten reason to do anything.

Keep those sticky notes handy. As you plan and direct your work flow, get used to the idea of using three rather than merely two categories: "Do it now," "Do it later," and "Do it never."

Deciding to "do it never" isn't at all the same as simply not doing it. If you toss it back on the pile and push it to the back of your mind, it will continue to clutter your physical and mental space, and it will need dealing with all over again. Make the decision not to do it—and tell anybody whose work is affected by your decision.

If it won't take long, and it doesn't interrupt something important, do it now. If it doesn't carry a high degree of urgency or if you have a task with a higher level of urgency needing your attention, do it later.

Don't let the medium of communication affect your decision. My e-mail announces its arrival with beeps and pulsating icons. The paper mail just sits on the desk. Even if I've turned my e-mail off, I get the beep and the blinking letter in the upper left corner of the screen. But that doesn't make the e-mail message more important than the paper message.

A ringing phone creates a heightened sense of urgency in many of us, but that shouldn't automatically give the caller a higher priority than the person sitting across the table.

If you decide to "do it later," note *when* you'll do it and *what*, specifically, you're going to do. If you don't, your attempts at organizing may degenerate into evasion instead.

PEELING OFF THE LAYERS OF PERFECTION: THE "GOOD ENOUGH" TENET OF TIME MANAGEMENT

You've decided to do it now. Now, how well will you do it? If it has to be perfect before you'll let it go, you've got a big time management problem.

I'm not advocating shoddy work or irresponsible performance. But I suspect that isn't really an issue here. Sloppy, irresponsible people don't read time management books. Conscientious people do. But the line between *conscientious* and *perfectionist* can be hard to find, and perfectionists have a tough time finishing anything.

The computer can make the problem worse. Because we can edit so easily, because we can always surf for more information, because we can run one more set of data at the push of a button, we may raise our quality expectations until we reach such lofty (and utterly ridiculous) pinnacles of perfectionism as "zero tolerance for error." (We might as well ban that horrible time waster, the bathroom break.)

How good is good enough? Who's going to see it? What are they going to do with it?

The meeting minutes that will be filed and forgotten need to be factually accurate and written in clear English; they don't need to be rendered in rhyming couplets.

The agenda for an informal meeting of department heads calls for a lower level of sophistication and polish than does the final draft of the annual report for the stockholders.

Working figures for the preliminary budget meeting don't need to be carried out to ten places past the decimal point. To the nearest thousand dollars is probably close enough, and more precise calculations are in fact a waste of time, since the numbers will all be changed later.

"Simplify, simplify," Thoreau advised us.

You can't flee to Walden Pond, but you can eliminate unnecessary tasks, delegate or swap others, and give each task an appropriate level of attention.

By managing your tasks, you'll be expanding the amount of time available to you.

CHAPTER 21

Whose Drum Do You March To?

I t's one of life's little ironies: by the time you get old enough to stay up as late as you want to, you're too tired to stay up late.

Just about every kid has fought to stay up past bedtime. You, too? If so, the more tired you became, the harder you no doubt fought the inevitable.

"But, Mom," you probably wailed with your last waking breath, "I'm not sleepy!"

You might as well have gone peacefully. You've spent the rest of your life living by the clock rather than by your inclinations.

LEARN TO KEEP TIME TO YOUR OWN RHYTHMS

In the "time before time," people lived by the natural rhythms of the day and the season. They got up when the sun rose, worked and played in the daylight, and went to sleep when the sun went down again.

But ever since Thomas Alva Edison finally found a filament that would get hot enough to glow without burning up, we've been able to defy the cycle of the sun, keeping ourselves awake with artificial light.

We awaken to the clangor of the alarm clock, yanking ourselves out of sleep rather than allowing ourselves to drift naturally up through the layers of sleep into waking. We hurtle out of bed and into the day's obligations, becoming estranged from our own dreams.

We eat by the clock, too, at "meal time," when it fits the schedule, or not at all. We combine work with food, to the detriment of digestion, with the "power breakfast" and the "working lunch" and the "business dinner."

If we become tired at the "wrong" time, like in the middle of the afternoon staff meeting, we fight off fatigue with caffeine or sugar or both, overriding our need for rest.

And we pay for it.

WHAT WOULD YOU DO IF YOU COULD DO WHATEVER YOU WANTED TO?

Most of us have developed a daily cycle involving one long block of time from six to nine hours of sleep and two or three meals, the largest coming at dinnertime.

You've trained your body to its cycle (or your own version of it) through repetition and reinforcement, but your body may show its displeasure, by being groggy and sleep-ridden at get-up time, queasy at dinnertime, wakeful at bedtime. You may simply struggle through these discomforts, or you may seek pharmaceutical help to rise, eat, and sleep at the "right" times.

Ever wonder what you'd do if you let yourself do whatever felt right? What if you had absolutely no obligations or appointments, a true vacation? You could get up when you wanted, eat when you wanted, nap if you wanted, stay up all night if you wanted.

You probably wouldn't do much too differently for the first few days. Our learned patterns can become quite entrenched. But after a few days, as you begin at last to relax and ease into a new way of life, what would you ease into?

What if you let the body, rather than the schedule, drive your day?

Scientists have wondered about such things. One experiment involves putting folks into an environment free of all obligations, free of all clocks and watches, even free of sunrise and sunset. Subjects had no schedules to follow and no clues as to when they "should" sleep and wake and eat.

Here's what they taught us by their reactions:

1. When left to our own devices, we will establish a fairly consistent pattern.
2. That pattern varies with the individual. One schedule does not fit all. What's "natural" varies from person to person. There is no one "right" way to pattern the day.
3. We like to graze. Rather than taking our nourishment in two or three major infusions, called "meals," we tend to eat smaller amounts several times a "day."
4. Sleep, too, comes in shorter segments. Rather than one large block of sleeping and one larger block of waking in every twenty-four-hour cycle, people sleep for shorter periods, more often.
5. The cycle isn't twenty-four hours long. Folks have their own built-in "day," and most of these natural cycles are a bit longer than twenty-four hours.
6. During each cycle, we have regular ups and downs. As anyone who has semi-slumbered through a meeting or movie well knows, not all states of wakefulness are created equal. Sometimes we're a lot more awake than at other times.

Attentiveness tends to undulate between peaks and troughs, and folks seem to hit two peaks and two troughs during each "daily" cycle.

SO, WHAT CAN YOU DO ABOUT IT?

Such findings seem to indicate that we're all living "wrong," in defiance of our own natural rhythms. Not much from this "natural" cycle seems applicable to the world of work and family and to the pattern set by clocks and calendars.

Let's take a second look. Perhaps we can make some adjustments, even while having to adhere to the basic outlines of the twenty-four-hour day and the five-day work cycle. Here are a few ways we can acknowledge, honor, and accommodate our natural rhythms.

HOW TO FIND YOUR RHYTHM

Your body has an inherent natural rhythm. To the extent that you can, you must rediscover your rhythms and live by them. Relearn how to listen to your body and recognize when you're tired or hungry or angry or restless, rather than override these feelings because they're "improper" or simply inconvenient.

We've all picked up opinions about diet and sleep, based on experience and inclination, study, folklore, and social pressure. Sometimes these four sources agree: you love apples, science says apples are good for you, and folklore teaches, "An apple a day keeps the doctor away." And aside from the scare over the pesticides, society seems to approve of apple eating. The only real drawback seems to be that Adam and Eve business, but even there, it's the serpent, not the apple, that does the damage.

Often, though, the four influences are in conflict. "Eat your spinach," your Mama and Popeye the Sailor told you. Scientists agree that spinach is wonderful stuff. But society has singled out spinach as the very symbol of something that's good for you but is really yucky, and, truth be told, you really don't like spinach.

Chocolate has gotten a bad rap (perhaps largely unjustly) for years, but lots of folks love to eat it, and it has come back into favor as providing at least some health benefits.

Smoking provides a more complex and troubling example. Most smokers start young, and peer pressure often plays a big part in getting started. Most beginning smokers react violently and negatively to their first few smoking experiences. From coughing to throwing up, the body does its best to repel the invasion of a foreign substance into the system.

If we persevere, though, the body learns to handle, then to enjoy, and finally to crave the smoke as we develop an addiction to nicotine. I've heard this addiction described by someone who would know as more powerful and harder to break than the physical dependency on heroin—powerful enough to keep people smoking even after they've developed emphysema or lost a lung to cancer.

Now science has established the causal link between smoking and these killer diseases to the satisfaction of most everyone except tobacco company executives. Twenty-five years ago the surgeon general slapped a warning on every pack of cigarettes.

Society has sent a mixed message. Ads for cigarettes originally touted the product as a health aid; athletes lent credence to this claim with their endorsements. As information from the medical community began to refute these notions, the appeal shifted to the cigarette as refreshment ("Take a puff. It's springtime"), social prop, status symbol, and image enhancer. (Marlboro didn't sell as a "woman's" cigarette with a red filter. As soon as they shed the red filter and started putting cowboys into the ads, sales took off.)

Back in the dark ages, smoking in public was for men—or fallen women—only. Then women gained "equality." ("You've come a long way, baby.") When the medical evidence against "secondhand," or "passive" smoke began to become pervasive and persuasive, many municipalities banned smoking in restaurants and public offices, and legal efforts to prevent sales of cigarettes to children intensified.

But already the pendulum is swinging back and the backlash for "smokers' rights" is being felt.

What have you decided about smoking? If you're a smoker or a recent ex-smoker, how many times a day do you have to decide? Have you decided that you don't really have a choice at all?

It's not as simple as just "doing what comes naturally." We initially repel the smoke but become hooked on it later.

It's not easy to know what's "approved" or "appropriate." "Society" says, among other things, that smoking is cool and that it will kill you.

But a combination of the body's initial reaction to smoking and a dispassionate review of the evidence on smoking and health can tell us what's right for us—even if we don't always do it.

Given the difficulties in knowing what's "right" and the inevitable clash between what our natural rhythms tell us and what socially enforced patterns dictate, you still might be able to alter your living pattern so that you're living more in harmony with your internal "music." Here are a few possibilities.

1. Establish a Fairly Regular Pattern

Many of us live by at least two different patterns, the work week pattern and the weekend pattern. We may reward ourselves with a late Friday and Saturday night, get up a lot later on Saturday and Sunday, and eat more and different things at different times.

Huge swings in patterns create constant disruption and the need for continuous readjustment. Shift workers suffer the most from its sort of disruption. Bringing the weekend and the weekday a little closer together may help you find and adhere to your true rhythm.

2. Eat When You're Hungry, Not When It's Time

Many of us have learned not to trust ourselves to eat naturally. We may have so thoroughly trampled our own natural sense of hunger and satiation, we're not even sure when we're truly hungry or when we've eaten enough. But short of suffering from an eating disorder, we can recapture—and trust—a more natural sense, an internal sense, of when we want and need to eat.

3. Take Your Nourishment in Smaller Portions

Grazing, noshing, snacking—whatever you call it, most of us do it, and feel guilty about it. But research indicates that grazing is a healthier way to eat than packing it all in once, twice, or three times a day. Insulin-dependent diabetics learn to eat several small "meals" a day. Some of the rest of us should try it, too.

4. Nap

We'll explore the subject of sleep in greater detail in Chapter 22. For now, suffice it to say that fifteen minutes of sleep or rest when you really need it is much more beneficial than the hours of "catch-up" sleep you get—or try to get—later.

5. Schedule by the "Rhythm Method"

Honor thy peaks and valleys.

One of the ways the human race seems to divide itself is the great morning person/evening person dichotomy. Some of us naturally wake up early and alert. Others do not. Some of us hit our creative and productive stride about 10 at night and work well far into the morning—or about the time the morning people are getting up.

Corollary to the great morning person/evening person dichotomy: morning people marry evening people. This is one of life's great mysteries.

But many of us, morning person or evening person, have to produce by the clock. Though both report to work at 9:00, the morning person is already hitting a midday trough, while the evening person hasn't yet become fully conscious. The system serves no one but the timekeeper.

Some escape by working at home or by seeking a vocation that more accurately reflects their inner rhythms. (Could a morning person become a jazz musician? Could an evening person find happiness as a morning drive-time radio personality?)

Most of the rest of us learn to adjust to the clock rhythm, but we all pay for it.

You need to discover your own rhythms and then accommodate them as much as possible. Keep a "mood log" for a week or two. As frequently as you can during the day, jot down the time and how you're feeling. Track your mood and your energy level. The mathematically inclined can create a mood scale, 1 to 10. English majors and my other numerically impaired brothers and sisters may feel free to use descriptors. It matters only that the notations make sense to you later.

After a week or two, see if you can discern your patterns, your peak and trough times during the day and the week.

When you find them, follow them as much as you can. Plan the tasks that require creative thought and clear decision making for your peak times. Leave the relatively no-brainer tasks for the troughs. (You may even be able to sneak in a nap here, but more on that in the next chapter.)

When you can't control the schedule (the big staff meeting invariably arrives just as your energy leaves), compensate ahead of time with a little extra deep-breathing, a longer mini-vacation, maybe a brisk walk. Compensate, too, by being aware of the source of your reactions. (The boss's proposal may not really be as stupid as it seems; you're tired and grouchy, after all.)

Learning and honoring your internal rhythms is one more way you can live a more productive, happier, and healthier life.

CHAPTER 22

Are You Getting Enough Sleep?

Y ou've probably never fallen asleep while giving a presentation to a large group of people—a horror brought on by a disorder known as narcolepsy.

But I'll bet you've nodded off while listening to one, yes? And I'll bet you've snoozed your way through more than one television program, school band concert, or movie.

You may have been reacting to an especially long, hard day. You may have been bored. But you may also be chronically sleep deprived. Should you be concerned? It depends on what else you've been sleeping through.

If you fall asleep every time you sit in one place longer than ten minutes, you may have a problem.

HOW MUCH SLEEP IS ENOUGH, ANYWAY?

Your mother probably told you that you should get your eight hours every night, and Mom's wisdom stood up for decades. But in the 1950s doctors began suggesting that we could and should get by on less sleep. One prominent article in the *Saturday Evening Post*, then a dominant synthesizer of American folk wisdom, suggested that only sluggards and dummies waste their time sleeping eight hours a night.

About that time the scientific study of sleep began (which makes it an extremely young science). We didn't even learn about a phenomenon known as REM (for rapid eye movement), the stage of sleep during which dreaming occurs, until about thirty years ago (a discovery that derived, by the way, from the observation that a dog's eyes move behind closed eyelids when it dreams its doggie dreams).

Sleep deprivation experiments (which must rank fairly high on the sadism scale) have clearly established that we need to sleep. Bad things happen when you keep folks awake for days at a time. But even here, the conclusions are murky, because some of the same bad things happen if you let folks sleep but deprive them of their dreams (another feat of cruelty accomplished by rousing sleepers every time they slip into the REM cycle but allowing them otherwise to get their "normal" sleep). After a few days of dreamless sleep, folks start having dreams, or delusions, while they're awake, displaying the symptoms of schizophrenia. (In case you're getting worried—you *do* dream, although you might not remember your dreams.)

But we don't know *why* we dream. For that matter, we don't even know for sure why we need to sleep at all. There have been lots of theories, but research has failed to bear any of them out. One compellingly logical notion, for example, posits that we sleep so that our poor hyperactive brains can cool off. But now we know that the brain is actually more active while we sleep. Different centers light up, true, but the brain certainly isn't resting.

On the all-important question of how much sleep we need, experts are divided. Some side with Mom, suggesting that most of us do indeed need between seven and nine hours of sleep a night, with Mom's eight a reasonable average. But others suggest that "normal" sleep varies widely with the individual. Thomas Edison is often cited as an example of a highly creative and productive individual who thrived on three or four hours of sleep a night (although revisionist biographers have suggested that Edison took a lot of naps, and some even suggest that his alleged nocturnal habits are folklore).

So, we don't know for sure why we do it, and we don't agree on how much of it we need. What *do* we know about sleep?

THE "NORMAL" SLEEP CYCLE

"Early to bed and early to rise," Ben Franklin admonished us, attributing a practical benefit if not moral superiority to the early start. But there is probably no "normal" sleep pattern or "right" time for waking up and going to bed. Folks have very different "natural" cycles; some are simply more alert late at night and have a terrible time trying to fight their way out of deep sleep when the alarm clock rips the morning.

Getting up at dawn may do the early bird a lot of good, but it's not so good for the worm.

Sleep itself is not a single, clearly defined condition. Sleep is actually a series of five stages of progressively deeper sleep, including the REM/dream stage. Most people will cycle through the five stages three or four times during an eight-hour snooze. The dream stages tend to get progressively longer during the night, and dreams will sometimes continue from episode to episode.

Lots of books purport to interpret your dreams for you, but no one has satisfactorily explained how *you* can have a dream that *you* can't understand. (The "right side" of the brain shows its murky, symbolic films, sans subtitles, to the literal-minded "left side" of the brain?)

Some claim to be able to see future events in their dreams, and most of us certainly revisit—and often reshape—the past in dreams. Others claim to be able to teach you the techniques for lucid dreaming (conscious awareness of the dream state and the ability to change the "plot line").

. . . and the Things That Go Wrong in the Night

1. Insomnia is by far the most well known and common disorder preventing you from getting your sleep, so common, in fact, that most of us will suffer from it at one time or another.

As the name suggests, *sleep onset insomnia* involves difficulty in falling asleep, while *terminal insomnia* (which sounds a lot worse than it is) manifests in waking up too early and being unable to get back to sleep.

Temporary insomnia often accompanies the presence of unusually high stress, and generally the insomnia eases when the source of the stress ceases.

Doctors advise simply riding out temporary bouts of sleeplessness. If you can't fall asleep or get back to sleep in a reasonable amount of time ("reasonable," of course, depending on the individual), don't fight it. Get up and do something else (but not something stimulating) until you feel drowsy. Then try again.

Force yourself to get up at your normal time, even if you've been awake for long periods of time during the night. If you adjust your wake-up time to try to compensate for the lost sleep, you'll prolong the insomnia. The condition will pass, and the short-term loss of sleep won't really hurt you.

If the insomnia is prolonged or even chronic, get to a sleep disorder clinic (which are sprouting like bagel stores across the country, a sign of our stressed-out times).

Recent research at these clinics suggests, by the way, that some "chronic insomniacs" actually get a lot more sleep than they think they're getting. Some even sleep a "normal" seven or eight hours but still report having been sleepless for most of the night.

2. During episodes of sleep apnea, the sleeper stops breathing for a few seconds. Many people experience mild sleep apnea every night with no apparent ill effects. However, some sufferers have several prolonged sessions each night, often waking themselves—and their partners—with a sudden gasp. Sufferers from severe bouts of sleep apnea will feel fatigued and logy, even after a "full night's sleep," and may find themselves nodding off at inappropriate times during the day.

If you—or your sleeping partner—are concerned that you may have sleep apnea, your physician can order an overnight sleep test called a polysomnogram.

3. Most of us also get the start reflex now and again, most often just as we fall asleep. Many report dreaming that they're falling, and when they tense, they "start" themselves awake. Again, a little is normal, but a lot is trouble. Rare individuals get the start reflex dozens of times a night, robbing them of sleep.
4. Folks suffering from literal dream disorder actually act out their dreams. Most of us don't keep twitching and starting and otherwise thrashing around during the night because of a little switch at the top of the spine that prevents us from acting out our dreams. But in rare instances the little switch doesn't work.

Dream that you're running a fly pattern, about to grab a Brett Favre pass and glide into the end zone, and you may leap and run into the bedroom wall—or even out the door and down the stairs!

You don't want this disorder to go untreated, in yourself or your roommate.

SO, WHAT SHOULD YOU DO ABOUT SLEEPING?

Most of us will never suffer from apnea, excessive start reflex, or literal dream disorder, and our bouts of insomnia will be short-term and self-curing. But experts now suggest that most of us aren't getting enough sleep. One report asserts that 33 percent of the American population is chronically sleep deprived. Short-term, this makes us cranky and less efficient. It may be a hidden factor in many traffic accidents. We don't know the long-term consequences because we haven't been studying sleep long enough.

SIX STEPS FOR GETTING A GOOD NIGHT'S SLEEP

If you encounter sleeplessness in the form of onset or terminal insomnia or both, you may be able to treat yourself with one or more of these remedies.

1. Avoid Nicotine, Caffeine, and Alcohol

Nicotine is a powerful stimulant. It's also addicting, and it carries harmful tars and other impurities causally linked to lung cancer and other life-threatening diseases. You're clearly better off without it. If you can't go cold turkey, try to avoid smoking within a few hours of bedtime.

Caffeine is also a powerful and pervasive stimulant, present in coffee and cola, of course, but also in chocolate and aspirin tablets and lots of other less obvious sources. Caffeine reaches its peak effect about four hours after you ingest it, so that after-dinner coffee at eight may be hurting your sleep at midnight.

Alcohol is certainly not a stimulant. In fact, it's a powerful depressant. It just doesn't feel that way, because the first thing it depresses is our inhibition. But it still belongs on the short list of sleep disrupters. That shot at bedtime may help ease you into sleep, but alcohol blocks your descent into deep and restful sleep.

2. Take Sleeping Pills Short-Term or Not at All

Sleeping pills and tranquilizers may help you fall asleep and may in the short term help you get through stress-induced insomnia. But these drugs have some serious drawbacks.

- They don't work for everyone, and even have the opposite effect on some, causing prolonged wakefulness.
- They, too, block descent into deep sleep.

- You may build up a tolerance, requiring larger doses to achieve the same effect.
- You can also become addicted to them.
- Worst case, you may wind up needing sleeping pills to sleep and stimulants to wake up, taking higher and higher doses of each in an extremely dangerous cycle.

3. Keep Regular Meal Times

Try to eat at approximately the same times each day, and avoid eating too close to bedtime. Digestion is a very active process and may interfere with your attempts to relax and fall asleep.

Nutritionists chime in with the advice that we'll process and use nutrients most efficiently by eating the big meal in the morning and then tapering off during the day and by eating several small meals rather than two or three large ones. However you refuel, regular habits will benefit healthy sleep.

4. Stick to Regular Bed and Rising Times

A regular sleep schedule—getting up and going to bed at approximately the same time each day—will help combat insomnia.

That means seven days a week. If you tend to follow one schedule during the work week but depart from it drastically for weekends, you may well have trouble falling asleep Sunday night and even more trouble dragging yourself out of bed Monday morning.

Folks who work split shifts have an incredibly high incidence of insomnia. The constant disruption is just too hard for most of us to adjust to.

5. Exercise Regularly

People who work out regularly report deeper, more satisfying sleep than their more sedentary brothers and sisters. Exercising on a regular schedule and not within three or four hours of bedtime is best for most of us.

All of this regularity may seem downright boring. But if you're having trouble sleeping, some adjustments here may enable you to solve the problem without drugs or other therapies.

But whatever you do, experts agree . . .

6. Don't Worry about It

There's nothing worse than lying awake thinking about how awful it is that you're not sleeping, how much you need that sleep, how bad you'll feel tomorrow if you don't get to sleep.

That is, of course, exactly what most of us do when we can't sleep.

Know that the occasional sleepless night is a natural reaction to life's stresses, and almost all of us will have our share along the way. If you can't sleep, examine your life for unusual sources of stress that may be causing the problem. If a specific problem or challenge is stealing your sleep, try the techniques we discussed elsewhere to diffuse your anxiety.

If grief is causing your stress, know that both grief and stress will abate with time, and with them your sleeplessness. Again, your reaction is perfectly natural.

IF SLEEPLESSNESS PERSISTS . . .

If you're concerned that a chronic lack of sleep may be robbing you of efficiency and alertness, hurting your relationships, perhaps even endangering your long-term wellness, first get a clear idea of how much and when you're actually sleeping now. Keep a record for a couple of "typical" weeks, noting when you go to sleep and arise, any naps during the day, and problems or disruptions in your sleep. Include subjective narrative, noting your impressions of how deep and satisfying your sleep is.

Also note your consumption of nicotine, caffeine, and alcohol and when you eat and exercise, since this all affects your sleep.

Now you're ready for a chat with a sleep disorders expert, who may have some immediate suggestions for you or may suggest an overnight stay at the clinic for a thorough monitoring of your sleep.

IS IT A PROBLEM OR JUST A PATTERN?

So, are you sleeping "right"? Is your pattern "normal," even if it doesn't fit the schedule Ben Franklin laid out in *Poor Richard's Almanac*?

For years a good friend and colleague of mine went to bed at 10:30 each night, awoke between 2:00 and 3:00 in the morning, read for about an hour, and slept again until 5:45. By my calculations, he was getting about six hours and fifteen minutes of sleep each night, and he certainly wasn't following any prescribed pattern.

He was also unfailingly alert and full of energy, a high achiever and a keen observer of life.

He may not have been "normal," but he certainly seemed to be thriving on his "abnormal" sleep pattern.

You may be an early riser and can't seem to overcome your tendency to be awake when most of the world is still in bed. Are you worried about it? Do you suffer any ill effects, or is your clock a little different from everyone else? It may or may not be a problem.

If you decide that you do have a problem, this chapter has given you the tools for understanding the problem, making some life changes, or perhaps getting some help.

CHAPTER 23

The War on Stress

"You know you're too stressed if you wonder if brewing is really a necessary step for the consumption of coffee." That's part of a puckish self-examination that circulated on the Internet recently. "You know you're too stressed," the "test" continued, if

- You can achieve a "runner's high" by sitting up;
- The sun is too loud;
- You begin to explore the possibility of setting up an I.V. drip solution of espresso;
- You believe that, if you think hard enough, you can fly;
- Antacid tablets become your sole source of nutrition;
- You begin to talk to yourself, then disagree about the subject, get into a nasty row about it, lose, and refuse to speak to yourself for the rest of the night;
- You find no humor in WASTING YOUR TIME reading silly "you know you're too stressed if . . ." lists.

Such satire never hits home unless it holds at least a kernel of truth.

Two social scientists named Holmes and Rahe created a more serious scale for measuring stress back in 1967. The Holmes-Rahe Social Readjustment Rating Scale assigned stress points to life situations. If you tallied 300 points or more on the scale within the last year, you were presumed to be at increased risk of illness or serious depression. Some of the events, with their point values, were:

- Death of a spouse (99)
- Divorce (91)
- Getting fired (83)
- Marital separation (72)
- Jail term (72)
- Personal injury or illness (68)
- Death of a close friend (68)
- Sex difficulties (53)
- Trouble with boss (45)
- Trouble with in-laws (43)

No big surprises here—but some serious omissions, according to sociologist Georgia Witkin. In 1991 she added new elements to the stress scale to more accurately reflect modern life in general and the evolving role of women specifically. Witkin's scale includes:

- Raising a disabled child (97)
- Single parenting (96)
- Depression (89)
- Abortion (89)
- Child's illness (87)
- Infertility (87)
- Crime victimization (84)
- Parenting parents (81)
- Raising teenagers (80)
- Chemical dependency (80)
- Son or daughter returning home (61)
- Commuting (57)

Great deal, huh? Stress depresses you, and then depression increases your stress.

Perhaps the only major surprise here is that "raising teenagers" only rates an 80. (800 seems more accurate, at least on the bad days.)

How about you? Can you tally 300 points or more, based on life events of the past twelve months? If you can, can it really make you sick?

THE PARABLE OF THE MICE IN THE REFRIGERATOR

Hans Selye is the founder of modern stress research. In one of his most famous experiments, he introduced mice to a stressful environment (in this case, the cold of a refrigerator) to see how they would react. Invariably, they went through three distinct stages. First, they fell into a funk, hunkering down to gut out a particularly long winter. (I went through a similar reaction during my first winter in Wisconsin.) But when the winter persisted, the mice went into a productive and cooperative frenzy, making nests and otherwise adapting their environment to make it more hospitable. (That's me, too, learning to put up storm windows and dressing in layers.)

Stage three really got Selye's attention and deserves ours. Almost without exception, the mice dropped dead. The cold wasn't lethal, but something about living under extreme stress for prolonged periods of time apparently was.

Subsequent researchers like Christopher Coe have made the connection. Coe separates baby monkeys from their mothers and measures the effect of this trauma on their white blood cell count. Take the monkeys from their mamas, and the white blood cell count plummets, thus depressing the immune system and leaving the monkeys vulnerable to all sorts of diseases. Reunite them, and their blood count rises.

THE FUN STUFF IS ALSO STRESSFUL

Another look at the Holmes-Rahe stress scale begins to bring the problem of stress into even sharper focus. Other items on the scale include:

- Marriage (85)
- Pregnancy (78)
- Retirement (68)
- Christmas (56)
- Addition of new family member (51)
- Vacation (43)

Wait a minute! Aren't those supposed to be the GOOD things of life, the events we work toward and wait for?

They are, but they're also very stressful, making huge demands of time and energy and requiring major adjustments.

Consider Christmas. All those preparations, the staggering expectations, the relentless requirement that you be happy! Most of us simply add this huge load to our everyday cares and responsibilities; life and work go on, Christmas or no. And just on the off chance that things don't go perfectly, you can add feelings of guilt, inadequacy, and remorse to the list of burdens.

Happy holidays!

But what about vacation—that oasis of rest and relief we struggle toward all year long?

You take on additional roles as travel agent, tour guide, recreation director, and master sergeant in charge of logistics. You exhaust yourself preparing for the trip while also trying to catch up and get ahead on your regular work. You leave familiar routines and surroundings behind for the unknown. So you're already hitting the top of the stress scale even before the first flat tire, missed plane connection, or botched motel reservation.

Are we there yet?

THE BOZO FACTOR

The world is full of bozos, and you're one of them. Don't get offended. I'm another one. We can't help it. We just keep getting in each other's way.

Put us into cars and we become particularly caustic. The guy who cuts you off in traffic stresses you. When you honk your horn at the offender, you stress the driver next to you.

Holidays, with their own sets of stressors, compound the highway insanity. "Driving probably will become even wilder now that Christmas (in P. G. Wodehouse's words) has us by the throat," George Will noted in a call for civility in the *Washington Post*. "Holidays and homicide go together like eggnog and nutmeg, so 'tis the season to study the wildness in the streets."

Relationship—or lack of relationship—inherently causes stress. Divorce is stressful (91 on the scale), but so are marriage (85), marital reconciliation (57), remarriage (worth 89 big ones on Witkin's revised scale), and—are you ready for this?—something Witkin calls "singlehood" (77).

Son or daughter leaves home and you get 41 nicks to the parental psyche. But according to Witkin, you get 61 points if your little darling moves back in.

You can't win. Enter into a relationship with another human being, get out of one, or avoid a relationship all together—you open yourself to increased stress no matter what you do or don't do.

List a few of the everyday things that people do to bother you, things like:

- cutting you off in traffic,
- emptying their car ashtrays in the parking lot,
- butting in line at the market,
- trying to buy more than twelve items in the twelve-items-or-fewer line,
- talking loudly during the movie,
- chewing with their mouths open,
- and on and on.

Petty stuff? Probably. But still annoying and stressful—and unavoidable.

STRESS HAPPENS

One more plunge into the stress scale to pick up another insight into stress:

- Change of financial status (61)
- Spouse begins or ends work (58)
- Change of line of work (51)
- Change in residence (47)
- Change in number of arguments with spouse (46)
- Change in eating habits (29)
- Change in sleeping habits (27)
- Change in recreation (26)

Lose your job or get evicted from your apartment? Highly stressful. But so is winning the lottery or moving into your dream home. The one constant here is change—*regardless of the nature of the change.* All change is stressful.

Which means, of course, that living is inherently stressful. Stress is inevitable.

You can't even buy your way out of stress. Psychologist Ed Diener's recent study indicates that higher personal incomes often bring their own set of stresses.

Little wonder, then, that a recent *U.S. News & World Report* cover story announced, "Stressed Out? You've got lots of company. But there are ways to fight back."

BEING BLESSEDLY STRESSED

You can't avoid stress. But you don't really want to.

Selye and researchers who followed him have learned that the total absence of stress is no better for you than too much stress. To remove all stress from your life, you would have to remove all relationships and all challenges. That probably explains why retirement rates so high on the stress scale. Yes, you shed the responsibilities and deadlines, but you also lose definition, purpose, a reason to get out of bed in the morning.

Selye coined the term "eustress" to signify the ideal compromise—not too little, not too much, but just the right amount of stress in your life. Your goal, then, should be to live in "eustress" as much as possible and to take especially good care of yourself during those inevitable times when you must exceed your safe stress limits.

But you may not be able to engage in safe stress by "fighting back," as that *U.S. News & World Report* headline suggests you do.

THREE GREAT LIES OF OUR AGE

We've declared war on stress. Time management is one of the weapons in our arsenal. Our battle cries include:

You can do more with less
Work smarter, not harder
A leaner workforce is a more efficient workforce
(thus the terms "downsizing" and "rightsizing")

You can put these bromides on the list of "Great Lies of Our Time" (right alongside "The check is in the mail," "I'll still respect you in the morning," and "I'm not selling anything. This is an educational survey").

You *can't* do more with less. You can only do more with more. If you're working more, you're doing something else (like sleeping and playing) less.

When someone advises you to "work smarter, not harder," they're telling you to produce more. They don't care if you have to work smarter *and* harder to do it.

A leaner workforce means somebody has to take on the work that somebody else was doing. If you've still got your job, that somebody is you.

Fight, manage, plan—do whatever you can to try to squeeze more work into the same limited minutes in the day—at your own risk. You're probably incurring still more stress.

So, if stress is an inevitable by-product of living, and if modern life puts us under ever greater stress, how can you possibly avoid taking on too much of it?

You probably can't, but you can *manage* the stress by understanding its nature.

THE FUNDAMENTAL TRUTH ABOUT STRESS

Stress isn't "out there" someplace, in the evil boss or the colicky kid or the traffic jam. Those are the stressors that trigger the stress.

Stress is inside you, your psychological responses to life's challenges.

Do what you can to mitigate the stressors, yes, but there's a lot you can't do anything about. You *can* do a great deal to modulate and modify your internal reactions, thus eliminating much of the stress if not the stressors.

You can learn to cope with life as it is—without letting it kill you.

You Have to Incur Stress to Lose Stress

Before you begin your strategic retreat from the stress wars, one final visit to the stress scale, where, nestled between "Trouble with boss (45)" and "Trouble with in-laws (43)" we find: Revision of personal habits (44).

That's right. Any attempt to modify your stress response is itself stressful. So you'll need to know that you'll feel increased pressure, not relief, when you begin to retrain some of your responses to stress. Don't get discouraged. This is normal and short-lived. You'll get through it, and the benefits will be more than worth the effort.

One Size Does Not Fit All

I'm going to suggest some strategies for reducing your stress level. You'll need to modify, adapt, add, and subtract depending on your specific responses to potential stressors.

Your stress response is different from anyone else's—one more element that makes you uniquely you. We have different tolerances for pain, different energy levels, different susceptibilities to and predispositions for various diseases—and different tolerances for stress. When folks like Witkin, Holmes, and Rahe assign points to various stressors, they are at best predicting the response in the "average" person—that strange being who makes $32,914 a year, has 1.782 children, and doesn't, in fact, exist.

You also have a unique perception of what is and isn't stressful. A round of golf on a Saturday morning may be relaxing for one and a frustrating endurance test for another. It doesn't depend on how good you are at golf so much as on how much you *care* how good you are. One person's party is another person's trial. Pay attention to what stresses you and then do your best to compensate.

And now, without further explanation or introduction . . .

HOW YOU CAN REDUCE YOUR STRESS LEVELS

1. Acknowledge and Honor Your Feelings

Some feelings seem unacceptable or even dangerous. Perhaps you've learned that it's not okay to be angry at your parents, to think less than respectful thoughts about your minister, or to lust after your best friend's spouse. You can deny such feelings, but you can't stop feeling them, and the process of denial takes psychic energy and creates stress. Feel what you feel. Then figure out how you should act—or not act—on those feelings.

2. Find Safe Ways to Express Your Feelings

Present your case to your supervisor, even if you don't think doing so will change that supervisor's decision. You'll have acknowledged and validated your feeling by giving it substance. (And your supervisor might even surprise you.)

Expressing feelings doesn't always help decrease stress, however. Rather than venting your anger, screaming at another driver in a traffic jam will actually increase the anger and your internal responses to it. You end up more, not less, stressed. In that case, you're a lot better off trying the next suggestion.

3. Unplug

You don't have to blow up every time someone lights your fuse. You can snuff out the fuse instead. How? Mom had it right; it really can be as simple as counting to ten. When you feel the anger flare, don't tell yourself you're not really angry (because it isn't "nice" to get angry). Don't rant, either. Take a deep breath and count (or laugh or spout nonsense or sing or whatever works for you).

But if you do that, you'll be letting that lousy driver ahead of you get away unpunished, right? Yeah, you will. But will screaming at him really "punish" him or "teach him a lesson"? You know it won't, and that knowledge will only frustrate you more.

Remember, too, that he's not trying to stress you out. He's not paying any attention to you at all; that's what's so annoying! He's just trying to get someplace in a hurry, just as you are.

And finally, remember that you're probably being somebody else's stressor, too. When I asked a workshop full of folks to list things other people do that annoy them, one person mentioned the bozo who crunches the ice in his soft drink at the movies. As I added the comment to our list, I silently vowed never to crunch the ice in my soft drink at the movies again.

If all that doesn't help you maintain your perspective, ask yourself this:

Is it worth making myself sick over?

All that churning inside really *can* help make you sick. And you're letting it happen to you. Do you really think "teaching" that "lesson" is worth it?

Don't get mad. Don't get even. Just get on with it.

4. Light a Candle

Getting annoyed at the sight of a mound of cigarette butts in the parking lot ranks high on a lot of folks' lists of annoyances. A lady in one of my recent workshops had a wonderful solution. She carries a "butt removal kit" —plastic sack, whisk broom, and pan. When she comes upon a tobacco dump, she simply removes it. Instead of getting angry and frustrated, she has accomplished something tangible to make her environment a little better.

5. Create Quiet Time Alone—Every Day

This can be nothing more than those mini-vacations we talked about earlier. But you may need more—a half hour to read or listen to music or do nothing at all.

You may *need* it, but you may not feel comfortable taking it. We spend so much time surrounded by other people and by almost constant noise, that silence and isolation can be intimidating. Don't be frightened of your own good company. Alone with your thoughts, you'll get to know yourself again.

6. Plan Your Escape Routes

When you check into a motel or hotel, do you immediately figure out how you'll get out in case of fire? You'll probably never find yourself in a motel fire, but if you do, your simple precaution might save your life.

Fire can break out in everyday life, too. Figure out how you'll escape when it does.

"When the going gets tough," Dwight Eisenhower once assured us, "the tough get going." This can mean, although I'm sure Ike didn't intend this interpretation, that if the going gets unbearable, you might need to get going—out the back door for a break before reentering the fray.

Will you find the courage to say, "Can we take a five-minute break here?" If you do, I guarantee others will silently thank you for it.

7. Wallow in Successes and Pleasures

Don't just check your accomplishments off the list. Acknowledge them—and the talent, energy, and determination they required. Don't just shovel in fuel. Enjoy the pleasure of the food.

8. Give Less Than 100 Percent

Giving 100 percent isn't even good enough anymore. With inflation, athletes must now give 110 percent. But nobody really has "110 percent" to give. You have limited time, limited energy, limited resources. You can't solve every problem, meet every crisis, rise to every occasion.

Some challenges don't deserve 100 percent. Save something for later.

9. Create a Third Basket

New tasks go into the "in basket." Finished work goes in the "out basket."

And some tasks should go in the "to-hell-with-it basket."

10. Do One Thing at a Time

One of the truly pernicious lessons of modern time management involves "multitasking," doing more than one thing at a time.

But we dilute the effectiveness of our work and rob the joy from our pleasures when we engage in multitasking.

We also show a fundamental lack of respect for others if we keep typing while on the phone with a friend or hide behind the newspaper when a loved one is trying to talk to us.

Talking on a car phone while driving can endanger more than a relationship. That sort of reckless multi-tasking can endanger lives—yours and others.

Watch kids at play. They are so focused, so rapt, they truly don't hear us when we call them. You had that power of concentration once. You can cultivate it now, giving full attention to everything you do. Don't try to spin ten plates on ten poles. Spin one plate really well.

CHAPTER 24

Don't Let Worry Rob You of Time and Energy

W orried about managing your time well?
You're wasting your time.
Worry steals your time and energy. It disrupts your rest, damages your ability to make decisions, and robs you of the pleasure and satisfaction you should get from work and play.

When you worry, you aren't planning, working, or solving problems. Worrying never resolves anything.

Worry ignores the present to fixate on a future that never arrives.

Worrying is like paying interest on a debt. You have nothing to show for it, you still have to pay back the principal, and you have no money left for the things you need. Substitute energy and time for money and you understand what worry really costs you.

We learn to worry, and we can learn to stop. We can replace worry with action.

THREE WAYS TO WORRY

1. A decision you must make: a big one ("Should I stick with the security of a regular paycheck or start my own business?") or a small one ("Should I order the double cheeseburger with fries or the salad with lo-calorie dressing?")
2. An action you must perform: like giving a business presentation or attending a social gathering
3. An event outside your control: like global warming or hostilities in the Middle East

Although the worries in the third category tend to be much larger in scope, they are also less immediate and therefore take up less of the worrier's psychic energy than do more immediate concerns, like the question of what to have for lunch.

Whatever you're worried about, you must realize that worry doesn't help.

MEASURING THE WORTH OF WORRY

1. Write down something you were worried about when you were a child.
2. Write down something you were worried about in high school.
3. Write down something you were worried about a year ago.

Now ask yourself these three questions about each worry:

1. Am I still worried about this?
2. How has the situation resolved?
3. Did worry help in any way to resolve the situation?

I'm willing to bet that in each case worry did little or nothing to help. Specific action may have resolved the situation, the passage of time may have eased or erased it, or you may have simply learned to live with it.

What are you worried about right now?

TEN WAYS TO GET RID OF YOUR WORRIES

1. Don't Resist or Deny the Fear

That only sends it underground, where it will fester and grow. It will return, stronger than ever, to attack you when you're most vulnerable. Face your fear. As you stop fearing the fear, it may begin to subside. If so, worry has already done its worst.

2. Name It as You Claim It

Sometimes fear comes disguised as the formless furies, vague dread or anxiety that can shake you out of a sound sleep and leave you wide awake until daybreak. Or it may take on a specific but false aspect. You may think you're worried about the coming congressional election or the sorry shape your public schools are in—laudable concerns, to be sure—when you're really worried about a mole on your neck that suddenly changed shape and turned red.

Give it a name. Write the worry down as specifically as you can. Now you can begin to deal with it effectively.

3. Consider the Consequences

Fear doesn't exist apart from you. Like stress, it's a reaction that takes place inside you. Since you created it, you can rechannel or diffuse it.

Ask: *"What's the worst that could happen to me?"*

If you eat that cheeseburger and fries, you'll consume about a week's allotment of fat, along with an enormous number of calories. This will not do you any good, and as a regular habit, it might shorten your life. On the other hand, the one meal will not kill you—and it will taste very good.

Perhaps you're worried about that presentation you're scheduled to give in two days. What, specifically, lurks under that general performance anxiety? Perhaps you're worried that you might make a mistake and, if you do, somebody might laugh at you.

Ask: *"Could I live with that?"*

You might not like it, surely, but you could certainly live with it. Now ask: *"What are the odds?"*

Have you been in similar circumstances? If so, how did things go then? Did you make a mistake? If so, did anybody laugh?

If you're still fretting . . .

4. Push the Worry to the Max

They won't just laugh at you. The laughter will turn to jeers. They'll start throwing things at you! They'll chase you from the room and out of the building! You'll lose your job, your spouse will leave you, and you'll wind up at the homeless shelter.

Naw. That isn't really going to happen.

Now, stop worrying, which accomplishes nothing, and prepare thoroughly for that presentation.

5. Figure Out What, If Any, Action You Will Take

You've got three choices:

- You can do something now,
- You can do something later, or
- You can do nothing.

Play with possibilities. You could eat the cheeseburger and fries now and fast for the rest of the month. You could compromise—single cheeseburger, with tomatoes and onions, no fries. You could eat the salad and steal bites of your friend's burger.

Actions you might take regarding the business presentation include: hitting the Internet to gather data; practicing in front of a sympathetic audience; faking a sore throat and going home "sick"; asking someone to make the presentation for you.

You may decide to do nothing because you feel that nothing you can do will help the situation or because the costs of any action you might take outweigh the potential benefits. Deciding to do nothing is quite different from failing or refusing to decide at all. If you examine the situation and decide there's nothing you can do, you'll remove the ambiguity and thus relieve a great deal of anxiety. If you evade the decision, you'll go right on worrying.

Perhaps you're worrying about a decision you can't make yet. If you're losing sleep over tomorrow's decision, tell yourself, "I don't have to decide that now." Repeat as often as you need to.

Now tell yourself, "Whatever I decide will be fine." Tell yourself often enough and you'll begin to believe it, not because you've brainwashed yourself but your intuition will recognize the truth of the statement. Whatever you decide really will be fine, because you'll act on it and, having acted, move on to whatever comes next.

6. Follow Through

If you've decided on immediate action, do it!

If you've decided to do something later, write down what you're going to do and when you're going to do it. Be specific: date, time, and place. Then be sure to keep that appointment. Otherwise, you'll soon learn to disregard anything you write down to do later.

If you've decided to do nothing, let it go.

7. Abide by Your Decision

Make each decision once. If you decide to eat the cheeseburger, enjoy the cheeseburger. If you decide on the salad, dive in. If you decide not to eat at all, savor the virtuousness of your hunger. Whatever you do, do it wholeheartedly. Resist second-guessing yourself.

Just because you've decided on future action or on no action doesn't mean the worry will go away. If it resurfaces in your conscious mind, send it packing, reminding yourself, "I've already decided that." Do this as many times as necessary.

This may not be easy. You probably have a long pattern of worrying, perhaps going back into early childhood. And you're probably receiving some benefit from all that worry. If nothing else, worry may be serving as a substitute for action or as a means of avoiding confrontations or evading decisions. Your worries may give you a sense of engagement with life, and you might feel quite lost for a while without those familiar worries. Work your way through this discomfort. You'll emerge with time and energy for doing instead of worrying.

8. Realize You Are Not Alone in Your Anxiety

You know your inner demons well, but you never see the demons others bear. You only see the composed masks we all wear in public. That fact may lead you to assume that others aren't worried. It isn't true. People worry; they just don't show it to you. Athletes call it "putting on your game face." We all do it to get along.

Other folks probably don't see *your* fears, either. They probably figure you're cool and calm—unless you choose to tell them otherwise.

9. Act in Spite of Your Fear

Don't wait for the fear to leave you before you act. It doesn't work that way.

Courage isn't lack of fear. Courage is action despite fear. Don't pretend to yourself that you're not afraid. Let yourself experience your fear fully. Then rechannel that fear into energy and alertness.

You will begin in fear, but soon a gentle calmness will replace that fear.

10. Protect Yourself from the Worry Contagion

The more you learn about controlling and redirecting your worry, the more aware you'll become of others' fretting and stewing. You may find yourself surrounded by colleagues who sing the "ain't it awful" blues most of the time.

If so, don't buy into their negativity and their false sense of urgency. Don't try to fix the worriers' problems. Don't try to argue them out of their worrying. Remove yourself from the blather if you can and let it roll off you if you can't.

THE FIVE FACES OF WORRY

1. Worry, Festering out of Ignorance

You can't imagine anything good coming from your present situation. You can only see bad options or no options, no way out at all.

Instead of worrying, learn. Seek information. You just don't know enough yet to see your choices, and worry is preventing you from even looking.

As new information allows you to posit possible actions, resist the reflex to reject any of them. Develop as long a list of possibilities as you can. When you've assembled your list, choose the best option or choose not to act.

2. Worrying Lurking in the Future

You're worried about a problem but can't do anything about it now, leaving you with no way to dispel your anxiety.

Instead of worrying, defer. Write down the specific time when you'll take action. Then set the problem aside. Every time the worry returns, gently remind yourself that you'll handle it at the appointed time.

3. Worrying Focused on the Past

"If only I had . . ."

"How could I have . . . ?"

But you didn't. Or you did. It's done or it isn't done. Either way, it's over.

Instead of worrying, release. Is there anything you can do to make the situation better now? If so, write down the action with the specific time and place you'll do it.

If there's nothing you can do, let it go. Don't wallow in regret. As fear looks to the future, remorse dwells in the past. They are the same crippling response facing in opposite directions.

4. Worry Feeding on Inertia

Action deferred can be worry compounded. The longer you put off the confrontation, the stronger your worry may become—and the harder it will be for you to overcome it.

Instead of worrying, act. Even a "mistake" is often better than doing nothing. If you can't act now, write down the action you'll take and where and when you'll take it.

Deal with it and get on with it.

5. Worry Thriving on Evasion

Decisions carry price tags. Whatever choice you make, it may cost you something. If you don't want to face those consequences, you may simply put off the decision. Your worry will rush in to fill the vacuum you create with your lack of action.

Instead of worrying, pay the price. Calculate the true cost of your decision as best you can—in time, energy, money, and damage to relationships.

When you decide on your course of action, decide also to pay the price—and then do so, promptly.

WHAT TO DO WHEN IT'S MORE THAN WORRY

The techniques we've outlined here will get you through most worries. But we need to differentiate between worry and a genuine anxiety disorder, such as obsessive-compulsive disorder or agoraphobia.

Between 1 and 2 percent of all Americans suffer panic attacks regularly, and as much as 30 percent of the population may experience at least one in a lifetime. Symptoms include dizziness and rapid heartbeat and may become debilitating.

People with obsessive-compulsive disorder receive unwanted thoughts they are unable to dispel and engage in repetitive behavior they are unable to stop. Such behaviors frequently involve cleaning (compulsive handwashing, for example) and checking (going back dozens of times to make sure the front door is locked).

Sufferers from agoraphobia (literally "fear of the marketplace") experience panic attacks in public settings. The condition may progressively worsen, until the agoraphobic can't leave the house, a specific room, even one corner of that room. Some become paralyzed for hours at a time.

These conditions stem from biochemical predispositions of the brain. Sufferers can't simply "snap out of it," and the steps outlined in this chapter won't raise anyone out of a genuine disorder.

However, a combination of medication and behavioral therapy most likely can alleviate or even eliminate symptoms. Get help if the fears get too big.

CHAPTER 25

Make Time
to Think

C reativity is one of the first casualties when we allow ourselves to get too busy.

You rush from appointment to appointment, challenge
to challenge. The phone rings—another disaster. You run faster
and faster to keep even—never mind get ahead. There's no time to
plan; you simply react.

In a moment of quiet despair, you realize that you haven't had
anything resembling an original idea in weeks.

Where did your creativity go?

It didn't go anyplace. You're still thinking. In fact, you couldn't
stop it if you tried. Go ahead. Sit in a corner and not-think for five
minutes. How about a minute? Five seconds? Can't do it, can you?
Zen masters need years of practice to learn to empty the mind.

Ah, but those aren't pearls of wisdom rattling around in your
poor, distracted head, you say? More like the rattling of loose
change in an aluminum can?

Listen closer. Your wisdom, your intuition, your creativity are
right where they've always been, just beneath the surface of conscious thought. You just haven't had time to listen.

You have almost infinite capacity for inventiveness and creativity. But when you get caught in the time trap, you leave no time for
reflection or for the incubation that yields flashes of insight.

WHY YOU SHUT YOURSELF OFF FROM YOUR GOOD IDEAS

Creative breakthroughs often derive from mistakes. Those ubiq-
uitous Post-it notes were one such "mistake," a glue that failed to

adhere as firmly as intended. Velcro was another flop, the military's attempt to create a fastener that could be "unzipped" without making any noise.

Often the "genius" idea comes disguised as irrelevancy. The folks at Pringles potato chips had no luck trying to devise a better bag for their chips, one that would keep the chips fresh and prevent crumbling. They found their answer only when they expanded the search from "bag" to "container" and began looking at crazy stuff like tennis ball cans.

Invention often comes from dogged determination, as when Thomas Edison tried out over seven hundred different materials before discovering that tungsten would glow without burning up when he allowed an electric current to pass through it.

How can you afford to try out seven hundred wrong answers? Maybe the question should be: How can you afford not to?

When you're busy, you stop seeking creative breakthroughs. You don't even welcome them if they somehow manage to thrust up through the wall of conscious thought and insist on recognition. Instead, you dismiss them as interruptions. You've already finished that project and need to get on to the next one. There's no time to go back and rethink it.

But instead of rejecting, you must embrace.

WELCOMING THE AH-HA!

The history of humanity is filled with dramatic creative breakthroughs.

Archimedes discovers the displacement theory while sitting in the bathtub one day observing the level of water in the tub fall as he stands and rise as he eases himself back into the water. Kekule dreams about a snake biting its own tail and discovers the structure of the Benzine ring after failing for years to discover it in the lab. Coleridge "writes" his "Kubla Khan" in a trance. Paul Stookey insists that he was the instrument, that his beautiful composition "The Wedding Song" played him and not the other way around.

Eureka!

Such breakthroughs come from the subconscious mind, which a man named Charles Haanel called your "benevolent stranger, working on your behalf." We all get them, but we may have shut ourselves off from them. To recapture the gift of inspiration even amidst the chaos of life, you must:

1. Listen. Create silence and time. Calm the din. Sit still, if just for a moment each day. Let your thoughts drift without direction.
2. Accept. Don't reject the idea, no matter how foolish it may seem. There's just no way to selectively welcome only the "good" ideas, the ones that are going to solve your problems. If you try to cut off the "bad" ones, you lose touch with them all and choke off the creative flows. And besides, you might not be able to tell a good thought from a bad one until you've lived with it for a time.
3. Note. When you receive a breakthrough, note it exactly as it came. Don't try to process, shape, apply, or direct it. Let it be what it is before you make it be something else.

CREATING THE AH-HA ON DEMAND

Can you really be creative on demand? You not only can; you have to.

Creative breakthroughs don't always or even usually come as surprise nudgings from the subconscious. In your world of constant deadlines and endless to-do lists, they are more often the product of a conscious process of problem solving.

You'll never find the time for this conscious process. No one will give you that time. You're going to have to *make* the time.

Here's a five-step process for making sure your creativity time yields the results you need.

Step 1: Make a Creativity Appointment

You've got a report to write, a presentation to prepare, a problem to solve. It will require more than just effort and time. You need inspiration.

Make an appointment to meet with that inspiration and do some brainstorming. I'm serious. Get out the calendar or the day planner and mark off a couple of one-hour sessions just for thinking.

If you don't schedule the time, you won't "find" it, and the thinking you need to do just won't happen.

Schedule that appointment at least a day and preferably longer ahead of time, and plan the session to coincide with a time of day when you're most alert and awake. Clear all interruptions.

Step 2: Tell Your Subconscious What You Want

I know of a top executive who took his staff on a working retreat to a ski resort. He held meetings with them all day Friday, and at the end of that time, he spelled out the problem to be solved at Monday morning's meeting, admonishing them to prepare thoroughly for the session. Then he turned them loose for a weekend on the slopes.

They, of course, gave the problem no conscious thought whatsoever—which is just what he figured would happen.

He knew that the problem would lodge in the subconscious of at least some of his advisors, and when the brainstorming began on Monday morning, they would surprise him—and themselves—with insights they didn't even know they had.

Such is the power of the subconscious mind.

You can bring that same power to bear on a "brainstorming session" of one. And you don't need a ski resort to do it.

Review the problem and the solution you're after. Be sure you've defined the problem clearly and specifically, but don't limit the scope of the potential solution. (You don't want a better potato chip bag; you want a way to keep chips fresh and intact.) Then put the problem out of your conscious mind. If you catch yourself brooding on it, send it back to the subconscious.

Step 3: Stay Alert

Every student of advertising has heard the story of the fellow who comes rushing into the tire store, clutching a newspaper in his hand.

"This is amazing," the fellow tells the salesperson. "Just this morning I decided to buy four new tires for my car, and here's your ad in the paper advertising your prices. What a coincidence."

No coincidence. The ad had been running in the paper for years. The fellow just never saw it until he needed tires, and then the ad jumped out at him.

Advertisers use this story to explain the need for frequency; if you want your ad to be effective, you have to keep running it. But it also illustrates a principle of selective perception. When your mind becomes focused on a topic, you begin to notice material relevant to that topic. A casual conversation overheard in the elevator, a remark made over lunch, a small item on the back pages of the newspaper, a report on the evening news—suddenly the world seems to be conspiring to feed you information to help you.

Along with the conscious research you may need to perform to get ready for your "meeting," stay open to information all around you that may prove helpful.

Step 4: Play with the Possibilities

It's time to think.

You've kept that appointment with yourself, keeping the calendar clear despite all the demands made on your time. You've done your best to make sure you won't be interrupted.

You sit at your computer, or you lie on a couch with a notepad and pencil, or you walk through a park with a tape recorder in hand.

All right, you tell your subconscious. *What's the answer?*

And nothing happens.

Now what? You've fought hard for this thinking time, and now you haven't got a thought.

Relax. You've got all the thoughts you need. Your subconscious isn't holding out on you. You just asked the wrong question.

Instead of seeking *the* answer, take a few minutes to try out as many answers as you can. Here are three ways to do it.

A. Play "How Many Ways?" Make a list of as many possible solutions or approaches as you can muster. Set a timer for ten minutes, so that you don't have to worry about the passage of time, and just let fly. Don't stop. Don't edit, evaluate, or in any way censor your thoughts. If something pops into your head, capture it on your list, even if it seems ridiculous. (I should probably say *especially* if it seems ridiculous.)

Remember Edison; there are no failures in the creative process.

"If you want to have a good idea," advertising executive Alex Osborne admonished, "have lots of ideas." (Osborne also coined the term *brainstorming*, by the way.)

B. Draw a "Tornado Outline." Write your subject or goal in the center of a large sheet of paper (or a whiteboard or flip chart or whatever you're comfortable with). Free associate key words, phrases, statistics, anecdotes, anything that seems relevant. Again, avoid censoring ideas.

When you're done, sit for a minute or so more, to see if any stray thoughts catch up to you. Then begin linking related material and numbering items, bringing order to the chaos. You now have a working outline for future work; the hardest part of the process is finished.

C. Create a grid. Return with me now to those thrilling days of yesteryear, when the resourceful masked man and his faithful Indian companion rode the range, bringing law and order to the Old West.

Fran Striker wrote a fresh script for the *Lone Ranger* radio dramas every week for years. He had great characters to work with and a durable myth of good and evil to develop each week.

But there are only *so* many pretexts for sending Tonto into town to get beat up, and only *so* many disguises for the Lone Ranger to don; after a time Striker began to run dry.

He didn't panic. Instead, he made lists—lists of weapons, lists of disguises, lists of settings, lists of bad guys, lists of all of the elements that went into his half-hour morality tales. He would then combine items from his lists, playing with combinations until he got something that seemed promising. This system kept the Lone Ranger riding for years.

This grid or matrix system works because inspiration often occurs when an idea or image from one frame of reference collides with an idea or image from a totally different context, creating something new, surprising, and original.

"Fellow dies and goes to heaven. There's St. Peter, guarding the pearly gates and eyeing him suspiciously. St. Pete checks his scroll, scowls, then squints down at the supplicant and says, 'Smoking or non-smoking?'"

One context, heaven, collides with another context, restaurant seating arrangements.

Inspiration "strikes" when the collision occurs spontaneously, which is to say without your consciously willing it to happen. But you can create the combinations consciously through the grid system.

Step 5: Stop Before You Have To

If you can't finish in one session, break while you're still in the midst of creating ideas and certain of where you're going to go next. If you wait until you're stuck or seem to have exhausted all the possibilities, and then stop, you'll carry a negative impression which can grow into dread and create a difficult startup time when you return to the project. But if you've left your work confident of your next steps, you'll come to the plan with a positive frame of mind and ready to resume immediately.

NEW AGE? NONSENSE

Lest you think this process sounds a trifle touchie-feelie, something right out of the hippie dippy 1960s, know that people like Charles Haanel were working with these methods at the turn of the century, and Dorothea Brande spelled out a similar process for writers in a book called *Becoming a Writer* in the early 1930s. This method is solid, it's time-tested, and it works.

By actually scheduling your thinking time, you'll nurture, maintain, and increase your ability to solve problems and develop new ideas creatively. As you do, you'll recapture a hyperalertness and an openness to possibilities, not just during those scheduled sessions, but during the rest of the time as well.

Instead of trying to find time to be creative or to fit creative thinking into your hectic life, you'll find yourself living in a constant creative state.

CHAPTER 26

Create a Values-Based Time Management Plan

"I wish I had spent more time at the office."
History has never recorded these as anyone's last words. I'm fairly sure it never will.

"I wish I'd spent more time with my family" is a much more likely deathbed sentiment.

List the three things in life that mean the most to you. Taken together, they might be your reason for living.

Here's how Americans completed that list in a recent national survey. The number listed next to each item indicates the percentage of people surveyed who listed it among their top three priorities. (So obviously the numbers add up to more than 100 percent.)

PRIORITY	PERCENTAGE
Family life	68%
Spiritual life	56%
Health	44%
Financial situation	25%
Job	23%
Romantic life	18%
Leisure time	14%
Home	11%

Got your list? Good. Now next to each of the three note the amount of time you spend on it each week.

Shocked?

If you aren't spending large chunks of time on the three elements you've listed as the most important priorities in your life, there are three possible explanations:

1. Important things don't necessarily require a lot of time.
2. You're mistaken about your priorities.
3. You aren't putting your time where your priorities are.

Let's examine each explanation.

DOES THE WAY YOU SPEND YOUR TIME TRULY REFLECT YOUR VALUES?

The Myth of "Quality Time"

Two strong social forces combined to move Harriet Nelson and June Cleaver out of the kitchen and into the workforce.

First, we began to require two salaries to keep up with our increasing material expectations. Today, nearly everyone owns an automobile (most households have more than one), and virtually all American homes contain a television. Three-quarters of U.S. households also contain a computer and cell phone. These are considered necessities rather than luxuries by half of Americans.

At the same time, women began giving public expression to the notion that being "just" a housewife didn't allow them to develop fully or to take their place as equal partners with men in society. They didn't just need jobs; they wanted careers.

As more and more former stay-at-home moms took jobs outside the home, their own expectations as well as those of society changed. "You can have it all" translated into "You must do it all."

Surveys noted that the distribution of housework didn't change in many homes even when the woman took an outside job. After a full day's work at the office, many women came home to another full day's work.

The term *quality time* was born.

As women joined their husbands in having less and less time for the kids and for their partners, social thinkers (i.e., freelance magazine writers) developed the theory that a little bit of very good time together would compensate for the lack of lots of time together. The more we talked about "quality time," the more we came to believe in its reality.

But "quality time" is a delusion spawned by guilt. Instead of "quality time," we simply have less time, and what time we've got is really "pressure time."

If you honestly believe that you can schedule a meaningful conversation with your adolescent son or daughter, or that lovemaking by appointment doesn't lose a little something in spontaneity, then you've bought the "quality time" concept. But relationships don't work that way. You can no more force a teenager to talk before he or she is ready than you can convince a cat to play Scrabble.

There's no hurrying or scheduling meaningful moments, breakthrough conversations, wonderful gestures. They occur in the midst of the muck, often when we least expect them. If you aren't spending time with a loved one, you're going to miss many of those moments. And you'll be putting much too heavy a burden on the time you do have together. "Quality time" turns into tension time.

ARE YOU MISTAKEN ABOUT YOUR PRIORITIES?

If you aren't spending much time on family or spiritual life or health maintenance, for example, then maybe these aren't really the most important things in your life.

Could you be wrong about your own priorities? Well, sure. In the incredibly complex interactions of conscious mind, subconscious motive, and psyche, we're perfectly capable of masking our true motivations from ourselves even as we might seek to hide them from or misrepresent them to others.

Also, the process of writing a list of priorities is different from the process of living your life. Your list could reflect the things you think of when asked to make a list, just as the opinion you give to a pollster might represent the opinion you would have if you had an opinion.

You might have listed the elements you think you're *supposed* to list, the elements it's acceptable or right to value most highly. You really wanted to list "making a pot of money" as your number-one priority, but somehow you just didn't feel right doing so. You knew that "family" was the "right" answer.

It's possible that you misrepresented your priorities—on a list that only you will see, in a book designed solely to help you make decisions about how you spend your time. It's possible—but it isn't very likely.

If you'd like to go back now and change your list to accurately reflect your values, that's ok. It's your list. But I suspect you got it right the first time.

Which brings us to the third possible explanation, that you aren't putting your time where your heart is.

WHY AREN'T YOU SPENDING TIME ON THE IMPORTANT STUFF?

Actually, there are three rather simple explanations, and none of them requires that you be a beast, a hypocrite, or a fool.

1. Time Spent Making Money Is Time Spent on the Family

We aren't just working for HD televisions and more cars. We're working to feed and clothe and educate our children, and to keep a roof over our heads. We're working so that the government won't have to take care of us. We're working so that we'll be self-sufficient even when we're too old to work (or we're pushed out of our jobs because of a mandatory retirement age). We're working because we're responsible and we want our kids to be responsible too.

If you're lucky, your vocation may also be an avocation, even a passion, helping you to grow and develop intellectually. You may enjoy your work and be able to share your accomplishments with your family. You may have been able to integrate your spiritual life and your work life. It isn't necessarily a strict either/or choice.

2. Working at Your Job Is Easier Than "Working at" Your Family

Jobs often consist of well-defined tasks. They aren't necessarily easy or even pleasant, but they're clear. You know what you're supposed to do, and you know what it's supposed to look like when you finish. Something outside yourself tells you when you've done well and when you need to work harder.

Knowing exactly how to "have a good family life" or to "be healthy" can be a lot harder, and the "product" of your efforts here is often intangible. You may be close to your family members, but you cannot control them, and that lack of control can be disconcerting.

3. Social Pressure Rewards Traditional Concepts of Work

Even when you begin telling yourself that other aspects of life are important, too, you can't slack off on the job expectations. Somehow you're supposed to devote more time to family without taking a minute from work—more of that "you can do more with less" nonsense, the underpinning for a belief in "quality time."

LIVE A VALUES-CENTERED LIFE

You aren't a monster or even a hypocrite. You're simply a time-pressured American without enough hours in your day for the important things in life. That explains it, but it doesn't fix it.

What can you do to make or find or create time for family, for spiritual growth, for health maintenance?

"There's right and there's wrong," John Wayne as Davy Crockett told us in *The Alamo.* "You gotta do one or the other. You do the one, and you're living. You do the other, and you may be walking around, but you're dead as a beaver hat."

If only life were that simple. But to do the right thing, you have to know the right thing to do.

Knowing the right thing to do, then, must dwell at the core of any real time management program.

Your values, your definition of the right way to live, are inside you. It's time to get them out so that you can live by them.

Step 1: Create a Personal Mission Statement

Most businesses and organizations have one—although the employees and members may be unaware of it. The mission statement is much more than policies and procedures governing day-to-day activities (though daily activities should reflect and contribute to the mission). The mission statement describes what the organization wants to be and what it wants to accomplish. Ideally, every member of that organization should contribute to building the statement and then should work to embody it.

What's your mission in life? Why are you living? What do you hope to be and do with your life? What values and assumptions underlie your core mission?

Spend some time with these questions. Let them dwell in your subconscious. Come back to them again and again. Be ready always to change and renew your answers as you grow in experience and wisdom.

Then you're ready to move on to a critical second set of questions:

- How will you act on what you believe?
- How will your life reflect your values?
- How can you live to fulfill your mission?

Step 2: Define Values in Terms of Actions

Let's suppose that, like two-thirds of all Americans polled, you listed "family life" as among your top three priorities in life.

What actions can you take—and what actions will you avoid— to live out that value?

Would you turn down an offer for a new job that paid more money if it required frequent travel and meant that you would be away from home for substantial periods of time? Would you rather be at home every night to help with your children's homework, bandage their wounds, play catch, or read them stories at bedtime? Is it more important to share duties with your spouse and have conversations, in person rather than over the telephone, that demonstrate your commitment to your marriage's future?

What does a commitment to "spiritual life" mean in terms of activities? It could mean going to church weekly (or monthly, or sometimes), reading and reflecting, participating in a prayer group, going on a week-long silent retreat. What does it mean to you? When you answer this question, you have created the possibility that you can live out this value in your life.

Step 3: Schedule for Your Values

If you don't get it on the schedule, it isn't going to happen.

That's the difference between a New Year's Resolution to "lose weight" and a Monday–Wednesday–Friday 7 A.M. appointment to take a spinning class at the gym.

Put it on the day planner. Be as conscientious about keeping that appointment as you would about an audience with the president or a quarterly evaluation with the boss.

Step 4: Go Gently into That New Life

Conscientious, yes. Firm in resolve and consistent in action, you bet! But judgmental and unforgiving, never! As you seek to change the way you live, remember one of the lessons we learned at the beginning of this journey: *all change, including changes in personal habits, is stressful.*

Old habits are hard to break, and daily life patterns are the most deeply ingrained habits of all. (To illustrate this truth for yourself, simply try putting on your pants "wrong leg" first.) You're going to forget, and you're going to slip back into the old ways.

You're also going to be overpowered by life at times, no matter how carefully you've planned and how well you've anticipated.

Don't berate yourself. Gently remind yourself and do differently next time. Slowly the new way will become the "right" way, the "natural" way.

Give yourself credit for what you do; don't just blame yourself for what you fail to do. If you finish fifteen of the seventeen items on that to-do list, rejoice in what you've done. Those other two items are what tomorrow was invented for.

Do one thing at a time, with all your energy, your attention, your heart.

And finally, with all the planning and evaluating and scheduling—don't try to do too much.

Time management isn't about maximizing the number of items you can check off in a day or a life. It's about living fully, productively, joyfully—by your definitions of these terms.

I'll end this with these words of philosopher/theologian Thomas Merton:

The rush and the pressure of modern life are a form,

perhaps the most common form,

of its innate violence.